Black Rood

THE LOST CROWN JEWEL OF SCOTLAND

DAVID WILLEM

Whittles Publishing

Published by

Whittles Publishing Ltd,
Dunbeath,
Caithness, KW6 6EG,
Scotland, UK

www.whittlespublishing.com

© 2022 David Willem
ISBN 978-184995-531-7

Cover image: a late tenth-century
Anglo-Saxon reliquary of enamelled
gold and walrus-tusk ivory,
provenance unknown. Copyright:
Victoria and Albert Museum, London.

Printed in the UK by Severn, Gloucester on responsibly sourced paper

To Z, R & F,

Thank you for your constant support,
wise advice
and unending encouragement,
and for everything else
you bring me.

Also by David Willem

Kicking, Following the Fans to the Orient
Saint Cuthbert's Corpse, A Life After Death

CONTENTS

PREFACE

This is the first time the history of Scotland's lost crown jewel has been told as a book-length narrative. I came across the story of the Black Rood just as I was finishing writing my first history book, about the remains of Saint Cuthbert in Durham Cathedral; and while I had vowed never to write such an excruciatingly time-consuming and challenging thing as a history book again, there was something about this story that I could not let go.

For half a millennium, the Black Rood – a cross-shaped reliquary of a supposed piece of the True Cross – existed as a symbol of an independent Scotland. Yet no collective national memory of it has remained. An echo of it has endured in the name Holyrood, and histories of Durham mentioned its connection to the cathedral and to the 1346 Battle of Neville's Cross near the city, but there is no remaining Scottish awareness of an artefact that had once been as central to the conception of Scotland at the Stone of Scone. This in itself made it interesting, but my uncovering of the story took place against the backdrop of the first independence referendum and debate about a second, and the more I found out about the Black Rood, the more topical and irresistible the story became.

As I got deeper into the research, I also realised that it was not alone. There was a Welsh reliquary of the True Cross called Y Groes Gneth, which had a similar history, and an Irish one, the Cross of Cong; and although these three crosses often had identical trajectories through time, they had never been considered as a triumvirate before, a realisation that made the telling of their collective story even more compelling.

Looked at together like this for the first time, the three royal crosses tell a new, estranging and symbolist story about Scotland, England, Ireland and Wales, and the relationships between them. And just at this moment, when the international alignments of these four countries are shifting more quickly than they have for centuries, this triumvirate of crosses also speaks about their orientation to supranational entities such as the Catholic Church and the British Empire. This confluence of themes became too hard to resist and I committed to writing another damned history book.

The fact that the three crosses were a triumvirate has also helped to structure the book as it helped to fill in the gaps in each history. The stories of the Black Rood, Y Groes Gneth and the Cross of Cong do not form three complete narratives. Each spends a portion of its time in darkness and obscurity, with long periods of penumbra when the reliquaries seem fixed in the institutions that house them, and then sudden moments of light when their presence is recorded and their appearance described.

So while we may know next to nothing about the Black Rood's origin and indeed its final disappearance, we do know about the emergence of the Cross of Cong into the world and what became of Y Groes Gneth, and their stories can be used to understand what might have happened to the Black Rood at the same time.

The stories of the Black Rood and its two cousins may not have been told together or in book form before, but they have been told separately by academic writers. I am indebted to three people particularly: to Dr Lynda Rollason, who first made me aware of the Black Rood, and whose writing on the topic in *The Battle of Neville's Cross* and in her wonderful new edition of the *The Rites of Durham* remain my go-to sources; on the Cross of Cong, I am grateful for the in-depth research that Dr Griffin Murray has undertaken in his book on the subject; finally on Y Groes Gneth (I have chosen to use the Welsh spelling of cross, 'Croes' or 'Y Groes'), I need to acknowledge the contribution of the late Winifred Coombe Tennant's work. I would also like to thank Simon Everson and Dr Helen Crampin for their separate, different but equally insightful criticisms of an early draft, and Dr Neil McGuigan for his writing and conversation about the Cuthbert community and King Malcolm III. I am also very conscious of the numerous other academics, many of whom I have namechecked on Twitter, whose work has influenced this book, particularly Dr Julianna Grigg and Dr Philippa Turner, who were working on the Black Rood at the same time.

Academic historians and writers of narrative history do not always appreciate each other, and I know some of the other side's gripes: the cherry picking for colour; the dearth of attribution and footnotes; the privileging of kings and queens over, well, the less privileged; the concentration on treasure-hunting over the accumulation of less scintillating data points; over-reliance on the evidence that exists rather than on an awareness of what has been lost. And I am as guilty of these charges as the prosecution is prepared to insist. (My team's gripes I might publish elsewhere but you can imagine what they are.) Therefore, for those academic readers who live in a cosmos beyond narrative, I offer this short paragraph as an abstract of four positions in the book which I think are new and worthy of consideration.

First, the Black Rood, the Cross of Cong and Y Groes Gneth should be considered as a class, and although I do not include them here, the Brussels Cross and the Enkolpion of Edward the Confessor might be included as possible English cognates. Second, it is worth reflecting on the possibility that Malcolm III really did finance the first phase of the building of Durham Cathedral, just as Holinshed's 'History of Scotland' claims. Third, that Edward III seems to have made parallel gifts in the aftermath of the battles of 1346. And finally, that the gold-and-garnet cloisonné cross found in the coffin of Saint Cuthbert in 1827 may have been hidden in the coffin during the Reformation rather than having been there since the seventh century.

Negotiating the opinions of academics is only marginally easier than trying to marshal the evolving perspectives of four countries that have been orbiting each other – sometimes in friendship, sometimes in union and sometimes in enmity – for many centuries. Relating these four national stories together at the same time has created artistic and political challenges, especially in this era of identity politics when who has the right to tell whose story has become a fraught issue. So I lay my background out here. I am Welsh by origin, with a Welsh orientation to England, but I pass easily for English, and I have written about supporting England in sport. I have also been lucky enough to take part in the life of communities within all four countries, and while in the cases of Scotland and Ireland these experiences have of course sharpened my understanding of Scottish and Irish perspectives and of the hard limits of Britishness, I felt I also needed the contribution of a Scottish editor and publisher to tell this story. I am grateful to Keith Whittles and his team at Whittles Publishing for their enthusiasm for this story and their contribution.

David Willem
Cork, Ireland
January 2022

PROLOGUE: THE FIRTH OF FORTH NEAR DUNFERMLINE IN 1068

The Black Rood came with her.

In that summer, two years after the disaster at Hastings, the remnants of England's royal family made landfall in Scotland. Their flotilla beached on the north shore of the Firth of Forth, an hour's march from Dunfermline, where the canny King of Scots had his citadel. They had sailed to Scotland to seek his aid. The last of England had come to Scotland to beg.

Tiny beneath the hills alongside the firth, the few dozen refugees left their ships to gather on the foreshore. They knew they were the last hope of their dynasty. They carried with them the heir and putative king, Edgar the Atheling. Hurriedly nominated to the kingship after Hastings by the council, Edgar was king by affirmation only. He had never been crowned. They honoured him the 'Atheling' because it meant throne-worthy, although sometimes they simply just called him 'the child'. He was not much more than sixteen-years-old.

Alongside Edgar came his widowed, aristocratic mother Agatha and his pious sisters Christina and, it would be said, the real head of the family, the devout, fiercely driven Margaret. And supporting them came the northern Thane Maerleswein and the last few earls of England who had remained loyal and alive. Together with whatever entourage of servants, attendants and retainers they had managed to bind to the remnants of their household, this was all the court the King of England and his family had left. They were the remnants of the court usurped by King Harold, killed at Hastings, and the remnants of the court that had surrounded his predecessor, the saintly King Edward, who had been so wrapped in religion that people called him 'the Confessor' and whose intestate death had led to Hastings. And they were the descendants of the court of King Edmund 'Ironside', Edgar's grandfather, and of all the courts, of all their ancestors, back to the great King Alfred who had cowered in the marshes to hide from the pagan Vikings, but who had fought back and, empowered by faith in Christ, had re-founded their dynasty, the House of Wessex, and made it the greatest in all England.

And now, like Alfred two centuries before them, their lot had dwindled to whatever they could carry. Without land, an army, even a crown, Edgar was throne-worthy in name only. All he had was his lineage and his daily-diminishing status to bargain with for whatever support the King of Scots might be prepared to give them.

Yet somewhere in their baggage – probably among Margaret's clothes and jewels, her books, keepsakes and finery – there nestled a treasure that told of the profundity of their past, and the potential for their future. They brought with them a cross-shaped reliquary whose gold and jewelled exterior was the counterpoint to the brutal simplicity of the thing it has been intricately crafted to hold: a portion of wood from the True Cross, a relic from the very tree that had been used to humiliate, torture and kill the Christ. They called it the Black Rood, and it was more redolent of their right to rule than any crown.

Edgar, Margaret, their mother and sister were among the very few souls in Christendom who could hold in their hands this chink into the eternal: a talisman that had been intimately connected to the Christ by the nails that had been hammered through His flesh. It was as profound a possession as they could conceive – a slither of the Passion that told how holy their dynasty was, how God-chosen the House of Wessex, and how assured their destiny. The world would open again before them, whatever the current desperation of their circumstances, because they were so close to the Godhead.

The family waited on the foreshore, lost in the vastness of the firth, readying themselves to meet the King.

1

MARGARET OF WESSEX, EDGAR THE ATHELING AND THE BLACK ROOD

Methought I saw a wondrous wood
Tower aloft with light bewound,
Brightest of trees; that beacon was all
Begirt with gold; jewels were standing
Four at surface of earth, likewise were there five
Above on the shoulder-brace.

The Dream of the Rood
(translated by James M Garnett)

There were witnesses to the dealings of the House of Wessex with the King of Scots. The servants, attendants and priests who fussed about them were always watching, and one of them would one day tell their story. He may not have been there with the royal family when they beached on the shore of the Firth of Forth that July day in 1068, but he would have heard the tales of this first meeting. He was a priest called Turgot and he would one day present himself as the family's personal confessor or religious advisor. A celibate young man in his twenties during his most likely period of acquaintance with them, Turgot had a butler's sexless devotion to Margaret, the Atheling's beautiful older sister. One day he would write her biography.

So it is this Turgot who tells us how, on learning that a small fleet of richly appointed ships had arrived on his shore, Malcolm, the King of Scots, sent his lieutenants down to discover what the visitors wanted. And it is Turgot, or one of the scribes who copied his writing, who records how Malcolm's representatives noted 'carefully… the nobility of the men and the beauty of the women'.

And when they returned from the shore to Malcolm's Dunfermline citadel, a tower high on a mound in the cliff-edged crook of a small stream, it is Turgot who has the lieutenants extol to their King 'the reverence of the older men, the prudence of the younger, the maturity of the matrons, the beauty of the young women, and the unity and diligence of the entire family'. One of Malcolm's men went even further. 'We saw there a certain woman', he said, 'who, because of her incomparable beauty of form, and the pleasant eloquence of her speech, and an abundance of other virtues, I announce this to you suspecting, in my judgement, that she is the mistress of this family, whose wonderful beauty and morality ought to be more admired than talked about'.

Malcolm cannot now resist coming down himself from Dunfermline to the shoreline. Apparently fluent in English and Latin alongside his native Gaelic, Malcolm may have spent a period in exile at the London court of Edward the Confessor and learned the language there. If that was the case, he would certainly have heard of Edgar, Margaret and their family, and perhaps even have met them.

Going down to greet them on the shoreline and asking how Scotland could help them, Malcolm, Turgot sniffily claims, put on airs for the occasion, acting 'more gently and comported himself more kindly'.

It would not have been difficult for Turgot's informants to see, as Malcolm unctuously offered Edgar and family his neighbourly, cousinly and un-refusable hospitality, what an opportunity was now presented to the King of Scots. Margaret had no land, no wealth and no dowry, other than what she and her attendants could carry. Yet she possessed something even more valuable: the future of the dynasty. If Edgar could somehow reverse the Norman conquest, any husband of hers would become brother-in-law to the King of England, and just as her brother was an atheling with a right to the throne of England, so too would be her children.

So what a prize it would be to have this princess locked up in his tower. Despite being well into middle age and possibly in an existing marriage which had already produced a son, the presence of the Princess Margaret opened Malcolm's mind to undreamt of possibilities. She could make him Malcolm III, King of Scots, brother-in-law to the King of England, or Malcolm III, father to the kings and queens of Scotland and England. And why not – father to the kings and queens of a united kingdom too?

In Gaelic, Dunfermline means the fort in the crooked line of water. Malcolm's tower, with its steep cliffs and natural moat, was said to be impregnable. Margaret wasn't.

One of the Anglo-Saxon chroniclers is snide about what happened. 'This summer the child Edgar departed', the scribe lamented, 'with his mother Agatha, and his two sisters, Margaret and Christina, and Maerleswein, and many good men with them; and came to Scotland under the protection of King Malcolm, who entertained them all. Then began King Malcolm to yearn after the child's sister, Margaret, to wife; but [Edgar] and all his men long refused; and she also herself was averse, and said that she would neither have him nor anyone else, if the Supreme Power would grant that she in her maidenhood might please the mighty Lord with a carnal heart, in this short life, in pure continence. The King, however, earnestly urged her brother, until he answered Yea. And indeed he durst not otherwise; for they were come into his kingdom'.

So, in return for sanctuary and perhaps even for supporting Edgar's attempts to reclaim their kingdom from the Normans, Margaret of the House of Wessex became Malcom III's new Queen of Scots. As his new queen, the first thing she did was to beautify the Dunfermline church where they were married. Not before, she would not want to presume on Malcolm's wealth, especially after she had protested so much; but she wanted to make sure the message went out that, whatever the fate of Malcolm's first wife, this was a marriage sanctified by God. So she furnished the church with vessels of pure and solid gold. She set her ladies-in-waiting to make and embroider the altar cloths, priestly vestments and other ornaments for Dunfermline and other churches. Turgot reports approvingly that no men were allowed to visit her ladies while they worked, except those she brought with her, and that even then 'no giddy pertness, no light familiarity' with men was accepted.

At last, these actions suggest, some resources with which to affect the world.

In Turgot's memoir of her, the couple are portrayed as a medieval beauty and the beast, in which a saintly and sophisticated young queen brings her coarse, oafish and unworthy husband to heel. Malcolm's nickname was Canmore – 'long neck' or 'big head' – and, whatever his skill with spoken languages, he remained illiterate. Big, thick Malcolm, less an anointed king of Christendom than a tribal warlord, or this is what Turgot thought. And, in his view, it was her role to tame Malcolm's brutish instincts in order to fashion a Christian king to queen it over – as if she were an antidote, or a benign Lady Macbeth. Turgot's anecdotes are all about her endeavours to domesticate the King and bring a feminine touch to his tower, the sort of life that any first-lady would understand: good works, charity, religious and ceremonial reform, interior design, fashion, and the rearing of heirs and heiresses. It was a world of interiors and of public appearances. The princess in the tower became a queen in her palace.

And when Malcolm appears to pay court to Margaret in Turgot's tale, it is only to laugh his bewildered laugh and shake his big old head.

'It was his custom to offer certain coins of gold upon Maundy Thursday and at High Mass', Turgot recalls, 'some of which coins the Queen often devoutly pillaged and bestowed on the beggar who was petitioning her for help. Although the King was fully aware of the theft, he generally pretended to know nothing of it, and felt very much amused by it. Now and then he caught the Queen in the very act, with the money in her hand, and laughingly threatened that he would have her arrested, tried and found guilty'.

Yet it is evident, despite all her good works, that Margaret had an ostentation which Turgot cannot conceal. Apart from covering everything she could in gold and silver or fine vestments, she introduced new fashions and luxury goods so that members of the court were said to have become like 'a race of new beings'. She also created a new, higher class of servant to act as an entourage for the royal couple on their travels.

Turgot protests that all this ostentation only derived from her being 'compelled to do as the world does', certainly the gaudy early medieval world. But he reassures us that, even as she walked in state robed in royal splendour, she was always mentally treading these trappings under foot.

She read and studied the scripture hard, or so Turgot would want to claim. One of her favourite books was a selection of well-known extracts from the gospels, the readings including the Saturday mass for the Holy Cross and those for Scottish saints. Yet even here she enjoys embellishment. When Christ speaks in her book, His words are garnished with gold lettering; the stories of the Crucifixion narratives have golden titles; and the large opening letters of the gospels are highlighted in gold.

Seeing all this glittering devotion, when the unlettered Malcolm realised that she preferred one of her books to the others, he too would begin to regard it with special affection. Turgot relates gleefully that, as Malcolm could not read, he would kiss the book instead, and often he would have it covered with gold and gems and then bring it to her as proof of his affection. Like a cat with the brightly feathered corpse of a bird.

'There was in him a sort of dread of offending one whose life was so venerable', Turgot observes, 'he readily obeyed her wishes and prudent councils. Whatever she refused, he refused also; whatever pleased her, he also loved for the love of her'.

In what could be her defining statement, she would one day advise an audience of clergy: 'You ought to do as we do'.

'No one dared say anything against her', Turgot murmurs.

Both Turgot and the writer of the Anglo-Saxon Chronicle marvel at the way her example affected a transformation in Malcolm, and it seems he was taken with the manners and mores of his beautiful, pious, sophisticated wife. In apparent gratitude to God, the Chronicle says, he 'wisely bethought himself, as he was a prudent man, and turned himself to God, and renounced all impurity'.

The celibate Turgot also wonders at the night-time exertions of the spirit he overhears. 'From her he learnt how to keep the vigils of the night in constant prayer', he explains, 'she instructed him by her exhortation and example how to pray to God, with groanings of the heart and exhortations of tears. I was astonished, I confess, at this great miracle of God's mercy when I perceived in the King such a steady earnestness in his devotion'.

Their first son Edward was born around 1070, named after Edward the Confessor, to mark him as an heir to the kingship of England.

Yet, despite the possibilities and the hope and faith in their choice of name, the Norman invasion was hardening into permanency. Malcolm kept his side of the bargain and supported Edgar's attempts to regain his inheritance: the first great pretender to claim the kingship of England from a Scottish stronghold. For four years, Malcolm helped his brother-in-law attack England, with Edgar even getting so far as capturing York. Yet, each time, he was driven back by William the Conqueror's strategic strength, tactical initiative and superior will. And Malcolm was far too canny to join Edgar in any direct tilting at the Norman war machine. Sure, he would invade the ambiguous lands between Scotland and England – Lothian, Northumbria, Cumberland – as long as it suited his own purpose of increasing his own power; he would resource his brother-in-law and wish him God's speed; and he would provide a base for Edgar to regroup after each failed incursion. But he does not seem to have gone any further.

By 1072, William the Conqueror had had enough. With southern England now under his rule, he pushed his counterattack into Scotland itself. Malcolm retreated before him, withdrawing towards the old heartland of his Gaelic kingdom, and so avoided the risks to both parties of a direct confrontation. In the end, the two kings had to parley.

The outcome was not in doubt. Malcolm bowed to William. Edgar was given up into exile in Normandy. Malcolm's son by his first marriage was offered and taken as a hostage. And Malcolm became, in the words of the Anglo-Saxon chronicler, 'William's man'.

And now that their hopes for the re-establishment of their dynasty in the Conqueror's lifetime had been set back so far, Margaret and Malcolm seem to have reached some equilibrium with their destiny. All Turgot's reports are of a queen who had made Scotland her realm. Next to the reedy strip of land where they first met, the couple sponsored a ferry for pilgrims to cross between the north and south bank of the firth: a North and South Queensferry. They were happy to live near the waterway that had brought them together and which linked their kingdom to the outside world. They seem to have focussed their court on Dunfermline and then moved it further south to Edinburgh. Baby followed baby – Edward was joined by Edmund, Athelred and Edgar – all Anglo-Saxon royal names, echoing the order of the last five Anglo-Saxon kings of England, and then by an Alexander, Edith-Matilda, Mary and, finally, a David. Nowhere do couples reveal their defining vision more than in the naming of their children, and Margaret and Malcolm were consciously giving the world future kings and queens of England. And when they had exhausted their appetite for Anglo-Saxon kings, they named their two youngest sons after the most militarily successful classical and biblical monarchs. They were not without ambition.

She was strict with her children, or so Turgot says. He likes to think of her as a mother superior, running her household like a nunnery; or perhaps this was the only model of female leadership he really had. He notes approvingly how she lined the children up for church, like so many baby monks and nuns, and, as the children grew, she seems to have chosen to complete her daughters' education by placing them in a nunnery in southern England, a kind of royal finishing school in Wilton, which may even have been run by her sister. For, whatever the disagreement between the King and Queen of Scots and William the Conqueror, Margaret's daughters were, unlike the usurper Harold, proudly royal and would be treated with respect, even in Norman England. Indeed, all her children inherited not only her deep faith but also her fierce sense of entitlement and her émigré's dream of a destiny merely postponed.

They were also to inherit the Black Rood. As precious a thing as only a true princess of Christendom could aspire to possess, this was the item from Margaret's dowry that most spoke to the legacy of the House of Wessex and the promise of the alliance with the House of Malcolm Canmore. A *crux gemmata*, or jewelled cross, the Black Rood was at once a crown jewel belonging to the royal and ancient lineage of Wessex, it was also an honour conferred by the pope, a witness to the Crucifixion, even an intimate of the Christ. The Black Rood embodied, in precious metal, jewels and sacred wood, how profound their destiny was.

For Margaret – educated, literate and pious – the Black Rood's embellishment of gold or silver signified the infinitely valuable, immutable and incorruptible nature of eternal life. The surface of the precious metal would have been studded with jewels and gem stones, and the colour of these precious stones would have tended towards the red, as this recalled the crimson sheen of Christ's coagulating blood as it glistened on the cross, testifying too of its preciousness to life while also signifying the purifying fire of suffering and death. The arrangement, number and size of the jewels would also have had meaning. Constellations of four jewels could have been arrayed around a larger central jewel or been placed emphatically on the arm-ends. This arrangement might signify the four gospel writers revolving around Christ, or how His message should be taken to the four corners of the earth. The five circling jewels might also encode the five wounds of Christ: one for each blood-rimmed nail-hole hammered through His hands and His feet, and one for the spear-wound leaking white and red fluid from the centre of His body.

She would surely have known the poem *The Dream of the Rood*, with its uncanny vision of a gold-clad True Cross as a shining beacon.

> *… I saw the glorious tree*
> *With vesture adorned winsomely shine,*
> *Begirt with gold; bright gems had there*
> *Worthily decked the tree of the Lord.*
> *Yet through that gold I might perceive*
> *Old strife of the wretched, that first it gave*
> *Blood on the stronger [right] side. With sorrows was I oppressed,*
> *Afraid for that fair sight; I saw the ready beacon*
> *Change in vesture and hue; at times with moisture covered,*
> *Soiled with course of blood; at times with treasure adorned.*

Whatever its exact form, as Margaret gazed on the Black Rood and meditated on its meaning, she would have experienced how the encrusting gold and jewels gave the relic a dual nature. Her mind would have moved back and forth between the rich immutable glitter of the embellishment to the squalid suffering of the crucified, corporal Christ who had been pinned to the wood it contained to twist in agony.

Possession of a portion of the True Cross was far more than just a focus of devotion, far more than a status-symbol or sacred souvenir. Margaret held in her hands a fractal portion of the True Cross, a version in miniature that partook fully of the power of the whole. And part of that power was its ability to act in the world. Just as the centurion, the two thieves, the disciple John, Mary, Christ and God had been agencies at the Crucifixion, the Cross too had been an equal witness and protagonist there. An intimate of the Saviour, the Cross had been honoured by being nailed to the Christ during His torture and death. And, like Christ, or Mary or Saint John, it could be addressed in the here and now, and it could speak. It was alive.

Far beyond mere literary personification, the Cross in the Dream of the Rood begins to speak.

> *A rood was I upreared; I raised the mighty King,*
> *The Lord of Heaven; I durst not bend me.*
> *They drove their dark nails through me; the wounds are seen upon me,*
> *The open gashes of guile; I durst harm none of them.*

They mocked us both together; all moistened with blood was I,
Shed from side of the man, when forth He sent His spirit.

And it could ward off evil.

Then need there no one be filled with fear
Who bears in his breast the best of beacons;
But through the rood a kingdom shall seek
From earthly way each single soul
That with the Lord thinketh to dwell.

The Black Rood, then, had its own personal and profound power. It gave Margaret and her family a line of communication with the Godhead. When she gazed on the relic, it might speak to her. The message of the Holy Blood would leak out of the pits of the nails and seep crimson through the dark drenched wood and out across the gold and jewels, dripping into their thoughts. 'On me God's Son suffered awhile', the Cross would whisper, 'so glorious now I tower to Heaven, and I may heal each one of those who reverence me'. Like Christ Himself.

And the way the poem talks of those 'who bears in his breast the best of beacons' suggests one more refinement. The Black Rood, Margaret's personal *crux gemmata*, might have been wearable, like a locket.

2

King Malcolm III, Queen Margaret and the Black Rood

Turgot's biography of Margaret was not his only legacy. His long career took him from court-confessor in Edinburgh to the priorship at Durham to the bishopric of St Andrews. But it was at Durham, with all the status and resources of its famous monastery, that he created his most enduring achievement.

Durham was beloved of the Anglo-Saxon dispossessed. The monastery Tugot now led had been founded by a community of monks whose history stretched back to the very establishment of Christianity in the remnants of the Roman province of Britain. The monastery had, through circumstance and strategic choice, become the inheritor of some of the most powerful traditions of the preceding 500 years, drawing together everything from the Irish hermetical piety of its founding saints and bishops, through to the renowned scholarship and manuscript collection of monks such as Bede, to its retention of some of the powers and status of the old Kingdom of Northumbria from which it had emerged, a kingdom which, unlike Wessex, had failed to survive the Viking invasion. All these traditions and legacies were embodied in the collection of relics that the Durham's monks had cherished and curated: the skull of their proselyting, founding patron King Oswald; the bones of Bede and the early bishops and saints; and, pre-eminently, the still corporal remains of the now-400-years-dead Saint Cuthbert.

It was this more than anything that attested to Durham's significance in the spiritual landscape of God's favour. Cuthbert had been one of the missionaries who had first taught the faith to the peoples of Northumbria in the seventh century. Eleven years after his death on the Farne Islands in 687, his fellow monks had determined to open his coffin in order to salvage his bones and place them in a reliquary. Yet, instead of the skeleton they had been expecting, they found his cadaver intact, even articulable, as fresh and lifelike as the day he had died. This miracle made the monastery at Lindisfarne famous, and the community of monks had cherished his unchanging corpse ever since, lugging his coffin with them as they fled the island to escape Viking attacks, carrying it with them across what would become northern England and southern Scotland, building biers for it in the places they sheltered, and founding churches for it in the places they settled, first in Chester-le-Street, and now, for the last hundred years, in Durham.

The corpse rested there in its church on a towering nub of rock surrounded by an oxbow gorge. Poised on the very threshold between death and resurrection, its healing, redemptive power emanated through the sides of the coffin, radiated across the oxbow gorge and transmitted itself to the surrounding lands and out into Christendom, bringing the righteous into its thrall and far off realms into its influence, its presence constant and felt by everyone.

Its power could easily be felt deep in southern England. The corpse of Saint Cuthbert and its community of guardian monks had an ancient, familial attraction for Margaret and the House of Wessex. They shared the same Christian Anglo-Saxon story. The royal dynasty had also been dispossessed by the Vikings and left with nothing. Like the fleeing monks, Margaret's forbear King Alfred had been reduced to hiding with the remnants of his court in the Somerset marshes. The religious community around the corpse and the house of Wessex thus shared the same epic narrative, first of terror and hopelessness, and then of resurgence and triumph as, protected by godliness, they had gained back more than they could ever have hoped. It was also the arc of Margaret's life.

The kings and queens of the House of Wessex had never forgotten the debt they owed to God for returning the faith they had placed in Him. When King Alfred's grandson King Athelstan completed his father's and grandfather's work and reasserted Anglo-Saxon rule across England, he came north to the house of Cuthbert to receive the saint's posthumous but nevertheless still active blessing, and to lavish gifts upon his shrine. This benefaction symbolised and celebrated this moment of national triumph and re-emergence, as the two remaining Anglo-Saxon polities, one centred on Cuthbert in the north and the other on the kingship of Wessex in the south, were reconnected to form a single realm. Athelstan's gifts were said to yet lie inside the coffin, arrayed on or around the corpse of the saint: a gospel book, a royal head-dress made of gold, priestly vestments with golden embroidery and rich cloths to cover and adorn the cadaver.

As the leader of the Cuthbert community, Turgot could see what greatness could be achieved with Durham's mix of faith, miracle, history, ethnicity and royal and divine favour. Working with the new Norman bishops, he saw that he could use the resources brought by the pilgrims to Cuthbert's shrine to build a new church for the saint: a glorious modern cathedral that would bring together all the peoples of Britain into a single multicultural community of faith, centred on

Durham, and in awe of Saint Cuthbert – a new mausoleum which might last a thousand years.

And thus it was to Malcolm, King of Scots, husband to a Wessex queen, that Turgot turned for the imperatum and likely some of the resources to build his new cathedral. And when the ground had been cleared and the foundation stone was ready to lay, it was Malcolm whom he invited to lay the stone.

Exactly a quarter-century after he had come curiously down to the foreshore to welcome Edgar and Margaret to his realm, the now 60-something King Malcolm came to Durham to establish a cathedral. Accompanied by the adult Edward, his eldest son with Margaret, Malcolm rode proudly south in the haughty manner she had taught him, like that of a continental king. Where once Malcolm had circled Durham as a border-raiding chieftain, now Turgot opened the gates and castle of the city before him and he entered as an honoured guest, a patron of a monastery, a founder of a great cathedral, a prince of Christendom.

On the cleared ground of the plateau on the nub of rock above the river, Turgot would have sketched out for Malcolm and Edward the airy lineaments of the vast imaginary superstructure above them, indicating the volume of sky the building would one day enclose. He would have walked his royal guests along the vast footprint of the building, showing them how, from the great west entrance to the apse in the east, the cathedral would stretch cliff-to-cliff across the whole island of rock within the deep oxbow gorge. He would have walked them down the long stretch of dark earth and exposed rock that would one day be the nave, perhaps discoursing how the new church was designed to have the same dimensions as St Peter's in Rome, and pointing out the siting of the arcades, the aisles and the plan for alternating piers and columns, showing them where the transept would cut across the east-west axis. Then, with more reverence, he would have brought them to the most sacred spaces at the eastern end, where the high altar and the shrine for Saint Cuthbert would be. Here Malcolm and Edward could peer into the hole that had been dug for the foundations of the new shrine and perhaps see exposed, fourteen feet below them, the bedrock of the plateau beneath. And perhaps it was here, at the holiest place, and with the unbuilt cathedral rearing in their imaginations above them, that they laid the foundation stone.

Margaret, of course, should have been there. If anyone had been the muse and funder of Turgot's audacious vision, it was Margaret of Wessex. But she had not been able to travel with her husband and son to repeat the homage of her forebear King Athelstan and to play her part in the foundation ceremony for the cathedral. Something ailed the queen. An agonising sickness had weakened her for months. At first, it had prevented her from riding out, and now it kept her to her bed, barely able to walk.

Turgot had visited her recently and helped her prepare her soul for death. 'Summoning me to come to her privately', he would recall, 'she began to recount to me in order the history of her life, and as she proceeded with it she shed floods of tears. In short, so deep was her compunction, and out of this compunction sprang such abundant tears, that – as it seemed to me – there was nothing whatever which at that time she might not have obtained from Christ. When she wept, I wept likewise; and thus we wept and at times were silent altogether, since by reason of our sobs we could not give utterance to words'.

Malcolm, Edward and Turgot, her menfolk united in their love for her, must have prayed for her in the presence of Cuthbert, asking the saint to intercede for her in this world, or the next.

The saint's coffin was boarded up in a great high-sided chest embellished with gold and jewels, and was displayed on a stand in a temporary shrine next to the building site. And it was surely here, closest to his pulsing presence and near to the gifts from King Athelstan, that King Malcolm III and the guardian monks of the new cathedral formalised the relationship that had been enacted by the laying of the foundation stone.

They did this through the creation of a covenant, a bond of co-fraternity, a sacred contract that laid out the spiritual obligations of the monks to Malcolm and his family and the family's philanthropic obligations to the community.

Whatever the gifts or promises Malcolm and Margaret had made to help build the new cathedral, the monks promised in their turn to keep this covenant of co-fraternity forever. They were to copy the text of this agreement into their Book of Life which they were to keep on the high altar when the cathedral was finished. The agreement stated that while Margaret and Malcolm were alive, that 'one poor man to be nourished daily'; that they and their sons and daughters should be 'partakers of all things that be to the service of God in the monastery of Saint Cuthbert'; and for masses and psalters to be said for their souls. The final clause of the agreement celebrated their 150 years of co-fraternity. 'Their anniversary shall be celebrated as an annual festival, like that of King Athelstan', the covenant stated. The terms could almost have been determined by Margaret. Perhaps they were.

But this was not all this state visit to England had prepared for Malcolm. After the stone-laying ceremony and the solemn oaths of the Covenant, Malcolm was joined at Durham by his brother-in-law Prince Edgar the Atheling for a royal progress into southern England. No longer a hope-filled boy on a beach, the intervening 25 years had made Edgar a royal man-about-town, a cosmopolitan gentleman and powerbroker, friend to the late Conqueror's son Robert Curthose and someone who could move smoothly between the Norman, Anglo-Saxon and Scots nobilities.

Long reconciled to the Norman reality in England, the brothers-in-law were to ride on together to Gloucester to greet the new King of England – William Rufus, son of the Conqueror – and to be welcomed by his court. With Edgar as diplomat and go-between, the two kings had arranged to parlay as peers. For while the peace that had been agreed with the Conqueror had broadly held, it had needed to be renegotiated and re-established several times with his sons. For Malcolm this had meant opportunistic, tactical incursions when the Normans were distracted, while the Normans had responded with strategic new castles and fortifications that created both new revenue and a defensible supply route from the sea that was edging ever closer: first at Durham and Newcastle, then Prudhoe, Tynemouth, Carlisle and Morpeth, and now even at Alnwick and Bamburgh. In this context, Malcolm's agreement to becoming a patron of the new cathedral was a reassertion of his interests and status. There was even the possibility that a new concord between the two kings might be recognised by marriage. The 37-year-old William Rufus had shown an interest in Margaret and Malcolm's teenage daughter Edith-Matilda, so they might even discuss the prospect of a marriage alliance between the two kingdoms.

Nevertheless, as they rode off towards Gloucester, with Cuthbert's benign influence on them and Turgot's vision of the new cathedral in their minds' eyes, it is not difficult to imagine Malcolm's hubris. He had become a pious Christian king, the equal of King Athelstan; his children and their descendants would inherit the Black Rood crown-jewel and the witness to the Crucifixion it contained; he was allied to one of the great missionary saints and had represented the House of Wessex at the foundation of one of the most ambitious building projects of the second millennium. It was the culmination of a 35-year reign in which he had drawn together his kingdom's Gaelic, Cumbrian and Northumbrian territories into a new, ethnically diverse and much stronger entity – a Scotland to match England. He would be known forever as Malcolm III, King of Scots, the founder of a great cathedral, husband to a Wessex queen, father by her of five sons and two daughters, and surely grandfather one day to kings and queens of a united kingdom.

Riding south in the company of his brother-in-law, the last Wessex king of England, Malcolm went to meet William Rufus not as a sub-king greeting an overlord, but as a peer and even – potentially – as a father-in-law.

But something happened when they get to Gloucester, some humiliating refusal by William Rufus to speak in person with him, some provoking failure to acknowledge Malcolm's understanding of his status, perhaps even a demand for homage as an under-king.

Malcolm returned to Scotland in fury. He had always been a pragmatist, and his pragmatism, patience and guile had meant he had been prepared to kneel before William the Conqueror. But in his sixties, he seems not to have found the will to do the same for the Conqueror's son, certainly not in England. Perhaps he was just too old, and now too proud.

The humiliation shocked him into action. He called on his army and, with Edward and his nineteen-year-old son Edmund, he led them towards Alnwick, aiming to disrupt the Norman encroachment there and to provoke William Rufus into a fruitless and expensive incursion, and then to a humbling face-to-face negotiation between equals.

Margaret, in desperation now, her illness incapacitating, begged them not to go. She was 'most urgent with him not to go with the army', Turgot reports.

But Malcolm, who had always obeyed her in all things, did not obey her in this.

She did not see him again. According to Turgot's account of the next few days, the news came back to Edinburgh that some treachery had occurred, and the army had been ambushed at Alnwick. Malcolm was killed outright, and Edward had died of his injuries, his body smuggled back to Scotland sewn up in the gut of horse.

No one in the court had the will to tell the dying queen what had happened.

But even on her sickbed, she would have known that something devastating had occurred. The servants attending her would have betrayed it, her physician would have known, her confessors, her priests, her ladies-in-waiting, in every gesture and stumbled word, would have leaked the knowledge. And the court outside her chamber would have been in chaos, because everybody would have been preparing for a period of insurrection or civil war.

It was not the death of Malcolm but the death of Edward that caused the turmoil. There was then no agreed understanding of an order of succession, no way of pre-nominating a second-in-line from among her other sons, no way of preventing other relatives prosecuting their cases with violence. Malcolm's brother Donalbain, or even Duncan, the abandoned son from the first marriage, might lead an anti-Wessex rebellion. Every close male relative was an atheling, and the succession of the kingship came down to who could secure the most support. But still no one told her, and, with each passing day, the imminence of the danger increased.

Four days after Malcolm's and Edward's deaths, Margaret emerged from her chamber. She managed to struggle to her chapel and take mass before she was driven back to bed by the pain. Her face began to noticeably whiten and she asked for her priests to stand over her and recite psalms. Then she requested the Black Rood be brought before her.

Something happened at this moment to the Black Rood. There was some delay in getting it to the Queen, some difficulty opening the case in which it was kept, or in accessing the Black Rood itself to reveal the portion of the True Cross within.

'Oh unhappy that we are', she cried out. 'Oh guilty that we are! Shall we not be permitted once more to look upon the Holy Cross?'

When at last the Black Rood was produced, she reached out to take it, hugged it to her and kissed its jewelled, golden surface. Then she used it to sign her eyes and face with the sign of the cross.

I may heal each one of those who reverence me.

She placed the Black Rood before her eyes and held it there with both her hands, waiting for the miracle of healing, or to pass through the agony of death to resurrection, to go through the nails and the wood to immutable life.

Outside the chamber, a decision was made. It is probable that she had to be moved. The court could not wait any longer for her to recover or to die. Enemies might soon be at the gates. One of her younger sons, possibly the nineteen-year-old Edmund seems to have been sent in, or he elected to go.

According to one of her priests, when her son set eyes on her, he was shocked into immobility, paralysed by the enormity of the moment. He saw the glittering Black Rood, clasped before her in fierce desperation, the nervous, watchful priests clustered at her bedside, the sheet-whiteness of his mother's face, her straining for death.

Seeing her son relieved her agony for a moment her and she rallied a little, asking for news of Malcolm and of her favourite, Edward, hoping that the thing she knew was not true.

Her son tried to tell the lie he had prepared, telling her that they were well.

'I know my boy', she said. 'By this holy cross, by the bond of our blood, I adjure you to tell me the truth.'

He could not hold his nerve and told her what she dreaded.

But instead of railing against Heaven at the death of her husband, the death of her eldest son, and the likelihood that everything she and Malcolm had achieved might now be threatened; instead, as was expected of a pious death, she thanked God, for giving her the depth of suffering that would cleanse her of her sins. She said a prayer before she died. Her face flushed red and white as her life ended. She held the Black Rood in her hands.[1]

3

THE OPENING OF A CATHEDRAL, DURHAM IN 1104

For 21 years after Malcolm and Margaret died, the cathedral they had founded rose. Quarryman extracted the sandstone from the cliffs and banks around the looping river gorge, chamfering its precipices into gentler terraces. The carters hauled the stone up to the centre of the rocky peninsular where the master mason directed the stone cutters in the slicing of it, the masons in the dressing of it, and the scaffolders in the raising of it up into the air. And, as its east walls on the plateau at the centre of the oxbow hill became higher day by day, the masons and the glaziers closed in a larger and larger portion of what had once been airy sky.

The cathedral rose, but not course-by-course as one building. It rose in sections as finances allowed, the holy east end which held the choir, the sanctuary and Saint Cuthbert's new shrine rose first, as was respectful. And in order to balance and buttress the weight of the rising stone, the cathedral put out offshoots, arching tendrils of mortared stone that took the weight of the east end and the central tower and transmitted it to the ground, the tendrils becoming in turn the arches within what would one day be the nave.

And when the east end of the cathedral was finished and the sky encased, the now elderly Turgot kept the covenant he had made with Malcolm and Margaret, that their sons and daughters should be 'partakers of all things that be to the service of God in the monastery of Saint Cuthbert'. Along with dozens of the most senior churchmen of his era, he invited the Scots royal family to Durham to attend the consecration of the new building and to bear witness to the moment when Cuthbert's coffin was installed in its new shrine.

But as the day drew near, and the pressure of preparations for the opening ceremony increased, the Norman monks in Turgot's charge began to rebel. Where, they whispered among themselves, was the proof that Cuthbert's coffin contained anything other than a bag of crumbling bones? Why should they rely on the word of these long-dead Anglo-Saxons and this old Anglo-Saxon Prior? After all, there had been no public demonstration of the miracle of Cuthbert's incorruption for many decades and certainly no one now alive had ever opened the coffin. The whispers grew louder, and the monks began to debate the matter more openly among themselves. Some believed that the coffin was now empty, but that the saint's virtues had lingered in its vicinity in a way that would account for the miracles of healing that still happened to pilgrims visiting the shrine. Others said that it was impossible to believe that a dead body, however blessed, could remain intact for almost 500 years without there being some kind of proof.

Turgot may have been in charge but he was now one of the few Anglo-Saxons left in the Norman monastery, and, with a new, unsympathetic Norman bishop grating against him, he, more than anyone, needed the miracle to be believed. His fellow Durham monk, the otherwise supportive Norman scribe Symeon, had already concocted a history of the shrine that presented the Anglo-Saxon guardians of Cuthbert as false-monks and womanisers who had cowered in the marshes before the Viking threat. The monastery, Symeon had argued, had been saved and cleansed by the coming of the Normans. It was only a short step to believe that the legend of the miraculous corpse now needed to be renewed or let go.

Even now, forty years after the conquest, the conflict between the Norman and the Anglo-Saxon histories of the shrine might lead to a demand that the coffin be opened, during the ceremony and in front of the dignitaries and the crowds that were already gathering. If that happened, if the coffin was opened with full prejudice by a cynical Norman and a mouldering set of disjointed bones were found, it would be a humiliation of everything Turgot had dedicated his life to, of the beliefs of Alfred, Athelstan, Margaret and of the House of Wessex, of the great Saint Cuthbert, and of all their piety, veracity and faith.

With the ceremony imminent and his diplomatic and architectural triumph at risk, Turgot took the last decision left to him. He selected nine monks, including the Norman Symeon and, five days before the opening ceremony, he went secretly to open Saint Cuthbert's coffin.

Carrying candles, iron tools and tapestries on which to lay out and wrap whatever they found, the ten monks slipped away after dark to avoid detection. They picked their way through the building site of the unfinished west-end with the open arches of the nave hanging uncannily above them.

In the vast black cave of the new building, they raised their candles and hurried through the choir to reach the shrine, where the great ornate case containing the coffin of Cuthbert had been placed in preparation for the opening ceremony, its gold and jewels glittering in the flickering light. They had already fasted and prayed in preparation, but now the ten prostrated themselves before the coffin. The weight of Cuthbert's corporal presence and his unending agency had manifested itself around them all their lives: through the daily respects they had paid to the shrine, via the many miracles of healing that occurred around it, in the reverence of the pilgrims, and through the authority and influence that their community had built up over hundreds of years. And now, for mere political expediency, simply as a riposte to Norman cynicism, they were going to open his coffin to check – to check – that the power they had experienced all their lives was real. Not only was this a blasphemous impertinence, the act of encountering Cuthbert's corpse was sure to bring them face to face with the awesome miracle of the resurrection, not a millennium ago and a thousand leagues away in the Holy Land, but in the here and now, via the still fleshy body of a 500-year-old man, his cadaver held in stasis by the purity of his soul's faith and by his favour with God. If it had dwindled away into inanimate horror and reeking corruption, it would destroy everything they had ever known.

The monks rose, resolved themselves again, lifted their crowbars and chisels to begin. But they could not stop their hands from shaking as they attacked the coffin.

The ornamental chest opened easily. Yet immediately within this first chest was a second: a great wooden casket covered in musty and tattered hides that had been nailed to it and bound with bands of iron. This surely was the weather-beaten, leather-bound coffin that had been used to protect the saint's body as the community fled from the Viking attacks. This casket was large too, suggesting another coffin must be cased up inside. The monks shrank back in fear.

Turgot ordered them back to the task, and when they did not move, commanded them again. This second chest was more difficult to open and the bangings and scrapings of their exertions echoed into the void. Finally, they forced its lid and found inside an even more ancient coffin, this one swathed in waxed linen and blackened with age. The lid of the coffin was carved and etched with old-fashioned images of a beardless Christ and the symbols of the four gospel writers: an angel, a lion, an ox and an eagle. They knew, or the historian Symeon knew, that this could only be the coffin from 400 years before, the one mentioned by Cuthbert's contemporaries. Everything was as they had been told. Surely Cuthbert lay inside.

Too scared and awe-struck to go any further, the monks had to be exhorted by Turgot one more time. Even then, they tried to escape the necessity of opening the final casing. They moved the coffin from the shrine behind the high altar into the middle of the choir. With the waxlight from their candles vanishing into the void, they tried to peek in through a crack, hoping to catch a glimpse of the body within. But in the end, they had no choice. They removed the coffin cover and stole a glance inside. There was yet another barrier, an interior shelf on which rested an ancient book of the Gospels. This surely must be the last layer. The shelf had two circular iron rings let into it and, eventually, they grasped them and lifted the shelf and could see what was inside.

Cuthbert lay in front of them, on his right side, whole. Surrounded and covered by bare bones and precious gifts, his robed 400-year-old body was swathed in bandages and wrappings, but still obviously intact. He even smelled sweet. He looked, they were to say, less like a dead man than someone who was sleeping. This was no humiliating wreck of mouldering bones but a miraculous demonstration of everything they and their Anglo-Saxon predecessors believed. The monks were in such awe that they all started back from the body, beating their breasts in wonderment. They fell to their knees. Symeon burst into tears.

When their shock had settled, they re-approached the coffin by crawling on their hands and knees. Reverentially they cleared the other sacred bones away and lifted the body out by its hands and feet. It began to collapse, to 'bend in the middle like a living man, and sink downwards, from its natural weight of solid flesh and bones', they would tell a contemporary. Someone rushed up to support the middle. They laid the corpse out on tapestries on the floor of the choir. Symeon held a candlestick and kissed the saint's feet.

Now they had removed the body, they could see a silk underlay on the base of the coffin. In the corners, and beneath the bones of the other holy men, it had begun to rot away. But where it had lain under Cuthbert, protected by the aura of the saint, the silk shone as brightly as the day it had been made. The robes too, in which he was swathed, were bright and as new. Nothing was besmirched by any trace of corruption. The miracle was real.

Having examined things to their satisfaction, and with the time of the midnight service approaching and knowing they would be missed, the ten returned the body to the coffins and placed them back in the chest in the shrine.

The next morning, in a full assembly of their brother monks, they shared the news. There was a long moment of incredulous silence as the doubters and the uncommitted adjusted their preconceptions and marshalled their demeanours to meet this new reality, and then the Norman monks broke into cries of synthetic joy.

The word went out. Cuthbert's body was whole. God's favour still lay on the shrine. The miracle endured.

* * *

It was Malcolm and Margaret's fifth son Alexander who represented their House at the opening ceremony. Following the power struggle after the deaths of Malcolm,

Margaret and Edward, their fourth son Edgar had, with the support of England's William Rufus, secured the kingship. But it was his younger brother Alexander, the heir apparent, who followed the footsteps of his father and eldest brother to Durham. He had been a young teenager when they died.

As Alexander and his entourage made their way south for the ceremony, the news of the confirmation of Cuthbert's incorruption would have reached and reassured them, and added to their excitement. The royal party would have been joined on the journey by pilgrims from the Scottish churches dedicated to Cuthbert for centuries. Alongside them came crowds of Anglo-Saxon churchmen and worshippers from Lothian, the sons and daughters of refugees who had fled to Scotland after the Norman invasion, some of whom had been made slaves and who had been freed by Margaret. As they passed through the lands that had once belonged to the former Kingdom of Northumbria, they would have gathered to them the people who still thought of themselves as the haelwofric – the people of the saint, the citizens of the polity in which Cuthbert was like an honorary lord. Together they created a single, roving, festive community that advanced on Durham. From the south came the Archbishop of Canterbury and his entourage, with other senior churchmen and more crowds of Anglo-Saxon and Norman pilgrims. All would have been eager to learn of a miracle that was not distant in geography nor ancient in provenance, but in their own land and of their own time. And as they drew near to Durham, they would have heard more details about what the ten monks had said they had found.

And just as his father and brother had arrived in Durham that fateful summer, so Alexander would have had the gates of the city thrown open before him and his childhood confessor Turgot would have been there to greet him on the plateau behind the walls. Except this time, rearing beyond him rose the sanctuary and choir of the new cathedral, the open arches of the unfinished nave looping the sky, and the north face and central tower rising to an inconceivable height that demanded awe.

As Alexander was guided through the crowds, Turgot would have explained that he had conceded that there should be a public display of Cuthbert's incorrupt body during the ceremony. His discovery had not ended the controversy, and the atmosphere was tense as the bishops and abbots, and the immense crowd of pilgrims debated the evidence among themselves. And with the expectation that they might soon witness or even experience a miracle, they jostled each other to get the best view.

It was Turgot who led the procession through the crowd and into the sanctuary of the new cathedral. He was followed by the Abbots of Séez, St Alban's, St Mary at York and St German at Ollesby. Alexander was given the highest precedence in the arrangements, apart from the personal chaplain to the Bishop of Durham and the Archbishop of Canterbury. Behind the principals came the forty other monks and clergy followed by yet more brethren of the church. The great procession progressed along the unfinished nave of the new cathedral and entered the building to gather in the new shrine area at the far east of the building.

The interior was a revelation. The assembly was in awe, its members stealing incredulous glances upwards to the concoction above them. This wide building was roofed with stone.

The vast walls led the eye to the broad arches of the ceiling. Yet instead of a roof made of joint-able, bend-able and forgiving wood, the stone continued upwards, curved inwards, became ribs that arched together and then vaulted across the impossible space. The stone walls did not end. They rose and met in the air. There was stone above air. It was as if Turgot had turned the nub of rock into a hollowed-out mountain.

The miracle they were here to attest had now been matched by the miracle above them, creating a more hallowed, more still and more eerie space. The canopy reverentially protecting the new altar and the new shrine was not a structure of perishable cloth or flammable wood, but one of immutable stone, suspended in air. It was the final and most dramatic encasement of the unchanging corpse, first swathed in cloth, then encased in wood and leather, and bound with iron: Turgot had wrapped Cuthbert's body entirely in stone.

The ceremony began. First, the assembly prayed. Then the coffin was laid out before them, and the lid and inner shelf raised. Turgot raised his hand, and, summoning his strength, with a 'tremendous charge' forbade anyone to touch the body except the Abbot of Séez, whom he had agreed should conduct the revelation of the corpse. Turgot asked Alexander and the other guests to 'make themselves acquainted with the truth by means of their eyes rather than their hands'. He asked his fellow monks to watch 'with a vigilant eye, lest anyone should be any means carry off even a particle of thread from the vestments in which the body was wrapped'.

Alexander could now look down on the 417-year-old, yet still obviously intact, mummified corpse, bandaged in its entirety. The head was swathed in a purple kerchief and, beneath this, was a gold jewel-studded royal headdress that, Symeon might have whispered to him, had been a gift from his forebear King Athelstan. Underneath these wrappings, the contours of the saint's eye sockets, nose, cheekbones and chin could just be seen.

Beneath the silks that had been wrapped around the body, Alexander saw that Cuthbert wore the vestments of a bishop. Overlying everything were the girdle, stole and maniple which had also been gifts from King Athelstan. These thin ribbons of cloth were richly figured with images of the pope and the saints, and were embroidered with gold wire and filled with bright colour: purple-red and green in the robes, with fawn mixed in for the hair, paler fawn for the faces, foliage in pink and sage, the lettering was myrtle green or pale purple-red. Nearby lay the book of the gospels that King Athelstan had personally presented to the saint 170 years before.

Beneath this, Cuthbert was robed in a loose, broad-sleeved vestment which opened at the sides like a tabard. A bright reddish-purple in colour, it was thick-woven with images of flowers and small animals, and interlaced with lime-yellow strands. The robe had a wide golden border around the neck and the arm openings, and the saint's bandaged hands were raised in benediction. Sandals shod his feet.

Lying to hand nearby, ready to be placed back in the coffin were the other treasures and relics Turgot had found: Cuthbert's ivory comb, reddish from age, a pair of scissors for cutting his once still-growing hair, a small silver altar which he might have used on his missionary travels, a paten for the bread, a small gold chalice for the wine – its base in the shape of a lion, an onyx ball on its back, and, finally, a skull, said to be that of King Oswald. Alongside them, three new covering cloths were placed ready to re-wrap the body when it was returned to its coffin.

And now the public demonstration began.

Alexander watched as the Abbot of Séez lifted Cuthbert's head with both his hands and twisted it back and forth to demonstrate how connected it was to the body. At one point, the Abbot took the head by the ear and shook it, and then, as a final act of bravado, he lifted its torso so that the mummy was sitting up and staring out into the assembled crowd.

Some of the monks could not bear to watch this manhandling and called out that he was insisting on more proof than was necessary.

The Abbot ended his demonstration and turned to the crowd.

'My brethren', he said, 'the body which we have before us is unquestionably dead, but it is just as sound and entire as when it was forsaken by its holy soul on its way to the skies'.

The congregation chanted the Te Deum in celebration. Alexander followed as the open coffin was hoisted on to the shoulders of bearers and, with the other relics and gifts going before them, and to the sound of singing, it was taken outside to be shown to the mass of pilgrims.

'The immense crowd', which was waiting for it in the bones of the unfinished nave, 'from very joy, burst into tears', said a contemporary historian of the ceremony, 'and fell flat on the ground, rendering it almost impossible for the procession to advance – all the while the voices of the singers were drowned by the strong cries of the praying, the exulting and the weeping for joy'.

4

KING DAVID I AND THE BLACK ROOD

The enkinging of Margaret and Malcolm's youngest son David took place at Scone in the spring of 1124.

David was the last of the three brothers to become king in turn. Both older brothers, Edgar and Alexander, had died childless. Margaret had raised her children to be like little monks and nuns, and the two brothers, perhaps in order to protect their family from fighting over the kingship, may just have taken this orientation all the way to celibacy.

David had been brought up at both the Scots and Norman courts. His older sister Edith-Matilda had fulfilled their father and mother's dreams and became Queen of England, though she had married William Rufus's younger brother King Henry I. On becoming Queen, she had taken David with her to the Norman court. While his older brothers ruled in Scotland, David had grown up and spent many years in England, becoming, like his uncle Edgar the Atheling before him, a sophisticated mix of Norman, Anglo-Saxon and Scot, with high expectations for what a king should be and what a king could achieve for his realm. There is a story of the young-blood Prince David happening upon his sister the Queen as she washed and kissed the feet of lepers, almost certainly in a conscious continuation of her mother's charity. The fact that the moment was recorded suggests that seeing his sister in good works was a revelation, an awakening of his conscience to the extent of his maternal dynasty's defining tradition of piety.

There was however something about the ceremony at Scone – something dubious or distasteful – that unsettled the sophisticated new King. His contemporary biographer, his steward Aelred, said of David's reaction to the ceremony that 'He so shrank from the national signs of subservience, which the Scots customarily show at the new installation of kings, that the bishops were hardly able to compel him to accept them'.

It is not recorded what it was in the ceremony that gave David such qualms, but the Scottish rite seems to have been far from the Christian norm. While a crown might have been involved, it is possible that David had to crown himself, as none of the Scottish bishops had the authority to place this symbol of a golden heavenly halo or garland of tormenting thorns upon the king-designate's head. And it wasn't an anointing, because the bishops had no papal licence to use the holy oil which symbolised the infusion of divine grace.

Records of a much later ceremony show how differently the Scottish version of the Gaelic king-making ritual had evolved from those of England and the Continent. Instead of validation by a bishop or archbishop, the central act seems to have been an election by peers, with the Earl of Fife having a hereditary role in bringing the new king to the throne while the kneeling nobles assented. This was then followed by an oration from a *shenachie*, a kind of bard, whose role was to extol the new king's virtues, to confirm his lineage and to add his name to the tradition: 'Hail King David, brother of Alexander, brother of Edgar, half-brother of Duncan, nephew of Donald, son of Malcolm, grandson of Duncan...' and so on and on, deep into the first millennium. The assent by peers and the confirmation of the lineage seemed to matter more than the priest.

And while the traditions of place mattered as much as the agency of a named archbishop in conferring legitimacy, it may have been the prominence given to the Stone of Scone that caused David's discomfort. Instead of the central rite taking place in the hallowed and still solemnity of a church, it seems to have happened outside – under the unsanctified and un-canopied sky, subject to the elemental caprice of the sun, the wind and the rain. And perhaps most disturbingly for him, instead of culminating in unction with sacred oil that had been blessed by an archbishop and so endorsed by the whole of church and heavens, the king-making power did not alight from above; it emanated from the earth, from below, from the very stone of Scotland. Even today, we can still hear the echoes of paganism – of something like a marriage between the king and his land. They must have reverberated even more strongly then.

Whatever the thing was that the bishops had to persuade him to ignore, it was strong enough for David's concern to be recorded by his biographer soon after he died. Even on his deathbed, no one forgets a bridegroom who had to be persuaded by the priests to come to the altar.

This king-making question was one that would come to haunt all of Malcolm and Margaret's Scottish line. What they wanted was papal authority for the bishops to anoint and crown them. They wanted a modern Christian rite that confirmed their vision of Scotland as an independent kingdom, equal with, and not subservient to, England. In Christendom, authorisation for bishops to validate and solemnise and a ceremony with crown and oil could only be given by the pope. But every time the Scottish royal family asked Rome for this right, their cousins in England successfully petitioned to prevent it.

This was to become a permanent affront to the dynasty's legitimacy and piety, and so to their fundamental sovereignty. Instead of the ceremony enacting the status of a monarch chosen by God, and that choice being consecrated by the church as befitted descendants of the House of Wessex whose faith-filled founders had rolled back the pagans, the Scottish king-making rite, at best, gave only a local legitimacy. At the worst, it was a humiliation.

This circumstance can explain the prominence given to the Black Rood over the next two centuries. It was Scotland's most significant crown jewel. While images on seals show enthroned and crowned Scottish kings clutching sceptre or sword, these may only have been tokens unsolemnised by the church. What was far worse was that it was possible that the crown they are wearing had itself been a gift from England's former King, William Rufus. He may even have placed it on Malcolm and Margaret's son Edgar's head in a ceremony at Melrose, in return for his support against the rebellion, and so symbolising the over-lordship of England. This was not satisfactory.

The Black Rood in contrast was unimpeachable. In possessing a portion of the True Cross, Margaret and her children not only had evidence of endorsement from Rome, they also had an intimate connection to the death on the hill at Calvary and to the only source of all Christian authority: the King of Kings. It was incomparable to any tiara gifted by England.

There is no hint that the Black Rood ever played any role in the inauguration of Scottish kings. But such a use is not impossible. Indeed, what else might a king of Scots of the holy house of Wessex swear an inauguration oath over, other than a portion of the True Cross brought to the country by the saintly Queen Margaret of that pious dynasty? And there are marks on the Stone of Scone that suggest it might have been etched out like an altar stone to receive a relic or reliquary.

And certainly, holy relics like the Black Rood were being used in this way on the Continent. The crown that was placed on the heads of the kings of Hungary was said to contain a part of the True Cross, and Margaret's children might have been familiar with this practice because Margaret's mother may have been Hungarian and she herself had grown up in the Hungarian court. In the same period, the Talisman of Charlemagne – a bejewelled circular gold broach on a gold chain with a hollow compartment containing a vial of the holy blood – may have been used in inauguration ceremonies for the Holy Roman Emperor. The Talisman had a polished, translucent and magnifying precious stone at its centre, allowing its possessor to see through its ostentatious surface and glimpse the visceral relic of the Crucifixion within. It was said to have been hung locket-like around the necks of Charlemagne's successors, like a chain of office.

Whether or not the Black Rood ever had a role in the enkinging ceremony, it is certain that David embraced the relic as one of the most potent symbols of his royal authority. Despite his reluctance at Scone, the reign of David I was to be vital to Scotland's development, and the Black Rood was fundamental to the new King's conception of both his kingship and his kingdom.

One of his first and most far-reaching acts was to found a new abbey to honour the True Cross. While hunting one day in the forest beneath Edinburgh Castle, the legend runs that the King, like Saint Hubertus, had a vision of a stag with a cross that materialised between its antlers. Taking this as a sign that his new abbey should be built on this spot, David called the new foundation Holy Rood. Like England's Westminster, the precincts of the abbey were to become in time a royal palace and then a parliament for his nation.

David's creation of a new institution dedicated to the True Cross was only one aspect of the conscious continuation of the work of his parents, and particularly that of his mother.

The youngest of Margaret and Malcolm's children, David was only nine-years-old when his parents and eldest brother died, and his sense of loss and respect appear to be the most profound of all his siblings. As had happened with his sister Queen Edith-Matilda, who had commissioned Turgot's biography of their mother, David's elevation to the monarchy gave him the resources to express that loss and respect in permanent form.

And just as his mother had taught his father and brothers, David venerated Durham. But instead of his merely paying his respects to Cuthbert's shrine by issuing a charter there or attending a ceremony as his royal brothers had, David went much further. He brought Durham to Dunfermline. He seems to have commissioned Turgot's master mason or the team of masons who worked on Durham Cathedral to build the great new abbey to replace his mother's matrimonial church. The same spirals and zigzags as Durham appear on the Dunfermline columns; the imposing south-east doorway at Dunfermline looks like the work of the same craftsman who carved the surrounds of the great south-west door at Durham; and the ambition of the project had the same scope as Turgot's vision – a determination to gather the swirling symbolic powers of a place and its meanings into a single monumental expression filled with redolence and intent. In David's case, his great new Dunfermline Abbey was brought into being to memorialise his mother, to serve as a royal mausoleum for his father, brother-kings, himself and his descendants, and perhaps even to provide Scotland with a new ritual space that was large enough and imposing enough to hold a coronation ceremony – a sanctified and capacious alternative to the *al fresco* sorcery at Scone.

David was to go even further. Such was his desire for Durham that he tried to make it part of Scotland. He tried to put his own man in as bishop. While England was distracted by a civil war over the succession of his niece to the queenship of England, David recaptured Cumberland and attempted to push the border with Scotland as far south as the rivers Tees and Ribble, arguably the most nearly successful attempt there has ever been.

David dedicated his reign to the fulfilling of his mother and father's ambition for Scotland. During 29 years of kingship, he introduced feudalism to the realm, and his pragmatic marshalling of his resources is a direct line of connection to his parents' dreams for their dynasty. He instituted a new legal system, endowed new religious foundations, created a royal mint, took control of the coinage, and introduced knighthoods and immigrant lordships, one of whom was his friend the Robert de Brus, the first Lord of Annandale. In the process, he became a king of European repute.

Even on his deathbed, in his final act as King, the now fifty-nine-year-old David emulated his mother. In May 1153, he was in his recaptured Carlisle when his health began to fail. In preparation for his end, he asked for the Black Rood to be brought to him, the reliquary important enough for it to be kept near the King always. It did not help him either.

'... when on Saturday his illness became more serious and the severity of his feebleness deprived him of his ability either to stand or to walk', writes Aelred, his former steward and biographer, 'he summoned clerics and religious and asked that the sacrament of the Lord's body be given to him. As they were preparing to bring what he had ordered, he forbade them, saying that he would receive the sacred mysteries at the sacred altar. He was therefore carried to the oratory on the hand of clerics and soldiers, and after the solemnity of the mass he asked that the venerable cross that people call "black" be brought for him to adore'.

'The cross, the length of the palm of the hand, was made with surpassing skill out of pure gold; it opens and closes like a box. In it can be seen a portion of the Lord's cross, as had been often proved by the evidence of many miracles. It bears the image of our Saviour carved from the most beautiful ivory and is marvellously adored with golden ornaments. The devout Queen Margaret, the King's mother, who sprang from the royal seed of the English and Hungarians, passed on to her sons as a hereditary gift this cross she brought to Scotland'.

'When the King had with utter devotion adored the cross held no less in awe than in love by all the Scottish people, and had made confession of his sins with many tears, he fortified himself for his death by receiving the heavenly mysteries'.[2]

David was buried in his new abbey at Dunfermline. The Black Rood he passed down.

5

TURLOUGH O'CONNOR, KING OF CONNAUGHT AND HIGH KING OF IRELAND, AND THE CROSS OF CONG

> By this cross is covered the cross
> on which the creator of the world suffered.
>
> *Inscription on the Cross of Cong*

The description of David's death is the only certainly eleventh- or twelfth-century description of the Black Rood. It was written by David's steward, the Cistercian monk Aelred of Rievaulx in a lament he composed on the King's death in 1153. Aelred describes the Black Rood as a solid-gold crucifix with golden ornamentation, the length of a palm, the corpus or body of Christ being made of ivory, and the whole opening 'like a box' to reveal the portion of the True Cross inside. This description also appears in versions of Turgot's 'Life of Margaret' that were copied after Aelred which means it is not clear whether the original description was derived by Aelred from Turgot or if it was sourced by another scribe from Aelred and then retrofitted into later versions of Turgot's 'Life'. An extant reliquary now at the Victoria and Albert Museum shows what Aelred's version of the Black Rood may have looked like (see the Cover Illustration).

Aelred had connections to Durham and, about twenty years after he was writing his lament, a Durham monk called Reginald was advancing a related claim.

Margaret, Reginald says, 'transmitted [willed] to Saint Cuthbert the cross, sparkling in a most wonderful manner with pearls and jewels, which even when dying she held in her hand.'[3]

Reginald does not state that this was the reliquary known as the Black Rood; and Margaret could have held numerous crosses on her death bed as she tried to gain relief from her agony. But Reginald's emphasis on the provenance of this gift and the family's role in the founding of the cathedral create the possibility that one of her sons, Kings Edgar, Alexander or David, bequeathed this cross to Durham, perhaps even in celebration of the fulfilment of their mother and father's bequest at the opening of the new cathedral. It also raises the possibility that the portion of the True Cross may have been placed in different reliquaries at different times and for different people and purposes, with each reliquary becoming what is known as a contact relic, retaining some of the status and some of the power of the True Cross it had once held. Aelred describes the Black Rood, as the 'venerable cross that people call black' as if there were something about the name of the reliquary that was no longer self-evident. Rood, related to rod, was the original Old English word for cross and it usually meant a crucifix, but it is possible that the 'black' in Black Rood may not have referred to blackness at all. It could be a legacy meaning from Old English, describing the bright, glowing shine from the transformed blackness of burning charcoal.

If there is any possibility that as well as the abbey, David also commissioned a new reliquary for the Black Rood, there was in Ireland a king like him who was contemplating the same profound circumstance at the same time.

In 1123, Irish annals record: 'Christ's cross in Ireland in this year, and a great circuit was given to it by the King of Ireland, Turlough O'Connor, and he asked for some of it to keep in Ireland, and it was granted to him and it was enshrined at Roscommon'.

This annal marks the appearance into history of the Irish cognate to the Black Rood. And unlike the arrival of the Black Rood in Scotland, which came as part of Margaret's trousseau, the gift and acceptance of the Irish piece of the True Cross was a deliberate symbolic act of recognition and honour for Turlough O'Connor, the new High King of Ireland. Although we do not know whether it came from the pope or another king, the ritual display of the gift across the country, the ceremony of its handover to O'Connor, and the resources and artistry that the High King would devote to its enshrinement were a demonstration that his power and authority were acknowledged by God and across Christendom. Turlough O'Connor, the first of the kings of Connacht to become High King and who would one day be called by the annals the 'Augustus of the West of Europe', now possessed his own piece of the True Cross.

And much like David and his developments at Holyrood and Dunfermline, O'Connor wanted to use the unimpeachable status of the relic to establish a new, national ritual and pilgrim centre at Tuam, in his Connacht homeland. This new religious centre could rival the established centres at Armagh and Cashel, and could then be overseen by his own placeman, a newly created archbishop for his royal precincts. And at the very gravitational centre of this scheme, O'Connor commissioned a new reliquary to honour and display his piece of the True Cross.

The craftsman O'Connor chose to undertake this commission was called Mael Isu MacBratain. Just as Malcolm meant follower of Saint Columba, so Mael Isu meant follower of Jesu, and Mael Isu may himself have been a cleric. He was the master craftsman in O'Connor's Connacht workshop, overseeing the creation of the crozier heads and staffs, crosses, chalice-like baptismal bells, hanging bowls, book shrines and all the rest of the panoply of devotion that O'Connor and his bishops required. Among Mael Isu's other prestige commissions were the honoured satchel-like reliquary for the Fiacail Phadraig (see the illustrations of the front and reverse of the Fiacail Phadraig) – the revered relic of Saint Patrick's tooth – and the large, traditional tent-shaped reliquary for the bones of Saint Manchan (see the illustration of the shrine of Saint Manchan), an Irish contemporary of Cuthbert. Dominated by two equal-armed crosses with graceful curving arms and a central boss that was itself complemented by four equal-sized roundels at each of the arm ends, with its five circling jewels, this reliquary of Saint Manchan was a *crux gemmata* of masonry scale.

We do not know how Mael Isu prepared to approach the new commission for a receptacle for the True Cross, surely the most significant of his life. We do not know how aware he was of the reliquary called the Black Rood, or whether he visited Edinburgh to examine that work and speak to the craftsman who might have contemplated a new reliquary for the new King David. Certainly, Ireland and Scotland had diplomatic relations. Edgar, David's bother, and Margaret and Malcolm's first son to be King of Scots, had sent Turlough O'Connor's predecessor and rival an elephant, perhaps even an elephant brought by Edgar the Atheling from crusade. And there are stylistic similarities between the Cross of Cong and other True Cross reliquaries such as the Brussels Cross that show that Mael Isu was well aware of the way that master craftsman from other nations had approached such a career- and soul-defining commission.

With the consent and perhaps the creative input of his patron the King and the presiding bishop, Mael Isu determined to make a tall, slim, processional cross of cast bronze and copper-alloy which were then embellished with all the gold and silver that O'Connor could provide (see the illustrations of the Cross of Cong front, centre and reverse).

Mael Isu's masterpiece was created around a wooden core made of two lapped pieces of ordinary oak. His first act was to carve into this core a simple, almost crude double-armed Byzantine cross: an act of personal, informal and ultimately invisible devotion which dedicated his work to God. To this core he pinned the cast sheets of bronze and copper alloy and began to embellish them with a rich variety of borders and overlying decoration – gold filigree, gilding, open-work panelling and inlays, set off by the black-inlay niello and punctuated by glass and enamel beads. With little touches here and there, Mael Isu referenced the work of earlier generations of Irish craftsman and the insular traditions that were now hundreds of years old: false binding strips suggested ancient construction techniques; the red and yellow of the enamels and the openwork casting on the reverse came from traditions that had been handed on to him. The saltire-shaped junction of the four panels on the reverse hinted at Byzantine influence.

Along the thin sides of the cross Mael Isu incised and highlighted in silver the name of O'Connor as High King, adding, also in Irish, the names of the new archbishop and the presiding cleric of the time, and finally inscribing his own name as maker. King, archbishop, priest and artist – all the representatives of Christ in Ireland had given their names to this holy work. And at the beginning and end of these dedications, Mael Isu also included a motto, this time in Latin: 'By this cross is covered the cross on which the creator of the world suffered'.

The dominant design of the Cross was zoomorphic, an Irish rendering of a northern European style in which a series of three successively elongating animal forms writhed about each other. Snakes, lizard-like forms and quadrupeds with stretched-out torsos, snaking limbs with lobe-like paws created a thicket of subtly asymmetrical filigree patterns that simultaneously possessed animal, vegetal and geometric qualities. Here and there, larger and smaller animal heads emerged through the surfaces of the Cross: on the side panels as pinheads surmounting the fixing nails; or guarding the saltire crossing at the reverse; or biting and clamping the shaft-end to the connecting knob and the knob to the socket-opening at the base. The effect of all this decoration was to capture the presence of an undulating life-force, an evolution from plant to snake to serpent to horse-like quadruped, the heads of fully realised animals thrusting from the plane of the Cross's surface, as if animated by the power of the Tree of Life within.

And at the front and centre of his cross, at the join of its arms, Mael Isu created a dominant circular boss above a conical aperture. And it was in here that he, or an attendant guardian churchman, would have reverentially placed the piece of the True Cross that the reliquary had been commissioned to hold. Like the Talisman of Charlemagne, Mael Isu had designed a circular removable setting above the aperture to hold a transparent dome of rock-crystal, convex beneath, which encased the relic and served to allow it to be, not only seen, but magnified. This final feature gave the True Cross an uncanny amplification of its presence and heightened the significance of the royal encounter with this witness to the Crucifixion within.

6

PRINCE LLEWELYN, KING EDWARD I
AND Y GROES GNETH

Margaret and Malcolm's great-great-great-great-grandson was crowned King of England on 19 August 1274. This new English king was the first of the Plantagenet line to be honoured, like the Scottish couple's slaughtered first born, with the now self-consciously archaic Anglo-Saxon name of Edward.

Tall, brave, pious, chivalric, jealous of his rights and quick to anger, this new incarnation of that ancient holy name was a paragon of thirteenth-century masculinity and kingship. Conventionally chivalric and conventionally pious, he stood a head higher than most of his male contemporaries and was determined to dominate everywhere he considered his realm and to lead Christendom as a crusader king. The quest to recapture Jerusalem and the Holy Land was the great adventure of his time, and he wanted to star in it.

Edward took the cross – as crusaders liked to describe their quest – when he was still heir to the throne. But this first expedition had turned out to be a disappointing and ineffective venture, achieving almost nothing. His allies and his own tiny army of a thousand men were struck down by heat and disease; and, instead of the keys to Jerusalem, the most memorable thing he brought back was the story of an attempted assassination – it was said that his wife Eleanor had sucked out the toxin after he had been stabbed with a poisoned dagger. Alongside this anecdote, Edward returned with a cadre of loyal lieutenants, a fascination with siege-defying castles, and, tellingly, a piece of the True Cross that he would wear around his neck in battle.

Edward had vowed to return on another crusade when he was king. But this was not a simple promise to keep. Much needed to be in place before any king anywhere could lead an army to the Holy Land that was capable of capturing Jerusalem. First, there had to be peace at home, as no serious combatant would leave a homeland in conflict. Edward's father's reign had culminated in a civil war, the so-called Baron's War, and the damage from this needed to be repaired before

Edward could return to crusading. Secondly, there had to be peace and stability in Europe in order that the combined power of Christendom could be focussed on the Holy Land. Finally, there had to be wealth and resources sufficient to maintain the crusaders while they were abroad. Edward therefore had a lot to do before he could become a crusader king.

One of his first tasks as king was to resolve was the fate of Wales, and its troublesome, over-reaching and disrespectful prince, Llewelyn.

Prince Llewelyn had played a canny hand during the Baron's War, aligning himself to the rebel Simon De Montford and becoming betrothed to De Montford's daughter. He had profited from Edward's father's weakness, using England's distraction to bring his complex, fractured realm into some measure of centralised order and even recapturing lands from the English marcher lords. Llewelyn's position as a player in English politics, his fame and his lands were greater than any Welsh leader since the Norman invasion.

But Llewellyn had a lot of catching up to do. The development of Wales since 1066 had been nothing like that of Scotland. It had had no equivalent of David I to modernise the country; it held no belief that it was a kingdom; and, without any culture of primogeniture, it was always unravelling into a patchwork of tribal territories that were overseen by bickering princelings who had little in the way of the resources of a modern state – the country more or less lacked money so could not easily be taxed. Nevertheless, it retained its own fierce certainty in the independence of its laws, culture and nationhood.

As the undisputed premier Prince of Wales, Llewellyn possessed the Welsh cognate to the Black Rood, Y Groes Gneth (see the illustrations of Y Groes Gneth). Of the provenance of this Welsh reliquary and its piece of the True Cross, hardly anything is known. Possessed by the princes of the House of Gwynedd, it flickers through history in different spellings, through French and Welsh and Latin: *la croice neite*, it was called, or *la croys neyt, crossneyht, groes naid, croes nawdd, crux neoti*. 'Naid', if it was 'naid', was Welsh for destiny, fate, chance, luck, fortune, or protection, sanctuary or refuge.

Like the Black Rood, Y Groes Gneth had been passed down from a deep, unrecoverable past. It was, some said, brought to Wales by Elen Lluyddog, the granddaughter of the Empress Helen who rediscovered the True Cross in the fourth century, and from which all the fragments were derived. Or it came, and perhaps even took its name from the Cornish Saint Neot who had lived in the ninth century. Or perhaps it had been brought back from a Roman pilgrimage by Hywel Dda, Wales's great lawmaker, in the tenth.

It was old though, its keepers knew that. And in shape, according to a late fifteenth-century image, it was in the form of a Celtic cross, with a circle joining the four arms, so quartering the space and ringing the central boss. The covering of the cross seems to have been sheet gold, and as a *crux gemmata* it was studded with the five symbolic jewels, one at the end of each arm, and one in the centre.

Alongside Y Groes Gneth, Llewellyn also sported the so-called crown of the first King of Britain, King Arthur, as symbols of his legitimacy and supremacy. But still he had refused to bring either item of regalia, or indeed himself, to Edward's coronation, where he would have been expected to pay Edward homage as his vassal. This was possibly just arrogance, or perhaps a misjudged attempt to use homage as a bargaining chip to secure his long-awaited marriage to the De Montford daughter.

After a couple of years, Edward had had enough. Llewellyn's calculated refusal to give Edward the respect and homage he felt he deserved was an unresolved political tension and personal insult that had to be redressed. And while Wales had remoteness, impenetrability and marginality from English concerns as forms of protection, Edward had learned the lessons of his father's weakness and occasional tinkering – that only resources properly brought to bear could defeat an enemy that was passionately independent and adept at guerrilla warfare. Like the gathering power of the optical lenses that were just being rediscovered and manufactured in Italy, once the undistracted power of the English state was focussed on his mountain kingdom, Llewellyn's game was up. The Prince was about to discover how seriously Edward took the notion of his over-lordship and the homage that derived from it.

Edward called up his feudal host, the loyal subjects who *were* willing to pay him homage and fulfil their military obligations to him. He raised an army of 800 cavalry and 2,500 foot soldiers. His quartermasters ordered up 200,000 crossbow bolts and retained the services of 360 harvesters to denude the Welsh of their grain supplies. Mustering in Worcester and then Chester in July 1277, and with a Roman legion's directness of purpose, Edward's feudal host and salaried soldiers cut a wide military road through the Welsh forests. His strategy was to encircle Snowdonia and starve Llewelyn out by cutting him off from the breadbasket of Anglesey, the summer isle behind the mountains and beyond the sea where the Welsh grain grew. Edward dispatched his harvesters there in September and by November Llewellyn had capitulated. The Welsh Prince gave the English King the homage Edward desired, first swearing fealty at Rhuddlan and then coming all the way to London to bend his knee in full public humility.

In an apparent celebration, Edward and his wife Eleanor attended a ceremony at Glastonbury Abbey to mark the re-interment of what were said to be the bones of King Arthur and Queen Guinevere. Edward had dominion over Wales and now he felt empowered to commune with the first, and very Welsh, King of Britain.

The royal couple co-opted the symbolic power of Arthur to the English monarchy, where it stayed.

Defeat did not, however, solve the problem for Llewellyn. To make Wales a modern state, he still needed towns and territory, with money that he could tax, and new territories with which he could reward his bickering princeling followers. In 1282 he rebelled again, because he had nowhere else to go, and this time Edward's retaliation was devastating.

With Robert Bruce, the father of the future King of Scots, among his retainers, Edward invaded with massive force. A bridge of boats – one of his monumental game-changing constructions that was so characteristic of his vision – was strung across the sea-strip of the Menai Strait between Snowdonia and Anglesey. The pontoon bridge collapsed, giving the Welsh one of their few moments of triumph as they watched the flower of English knighthood pulled by their armour beneath the waves. But it was over for Llewellyn before it began. Starved out for a second time, he is said to have tried to make a desperate break to escape Snowdonia. The last native Prince of Wales was brought down shouting out his own name, presumably in an attempt to save himself for ransom, but was decapitated.

Edward was exultant. As the first modern King to incarnate the role of King Arthur, High King of all Britain, he commissioned an appropriate triumph to honour his achievement. Although records of the occasion no longer exist, it was some kind of round-table extravaganza held at Nefyn on the Llyn peninsular. Edward took for himself the Crown of Arthur and even had Llewelyn's seal matrices melted down into a chalice – a grail-cup – from which he and the knights of his round table could drink his health.

Afterwards, Edward went on a grand, leisurely tour of his new domain. He took in Harlech, Caernarfon and Conway, and made a point of staying at Llewelyn's royal residences – pissing in the Prince's privies. In mocking humiliation, the rest of Llewelyn's treasure was melted down into plate so Edward and his court could eat off it.

And as he progressed around Wales in triumph that summer, Edward would have begun to plan, in his mind's eye, the encircling ring of castles that would come to define Wales and its new relationship with England.

Designed to be supplied from the sea or from specially constructed canals, and using the latest siege-defying facilities, Edward's castles at Caernarfon, Conway, Harlech, Rhuddlan and Beaumaris would not be mere brutalist, technical emanations of power. Certainly, Edward loved the mechanics of thirteenth-century warfare. He was a chivalric technocrat and revelled in his command of supply lines, pontoon bridges, siege engines, castles and battalions of sappers. But he also has a taste for the symbolism of dominion.

The whole texture of his mind was symbolist – idealist, mystical, spiritual. If reality was too prosaic, he would enhance it; and the ring of imposing castles he would build around Llewellyn's tiny mountain fiefdom was patently disproportionate. Were the nephew and nieces, and the daughter of Llewelyn, all of whom Edward had had imprisoned, really going to escape and build the Welsh towns that would allow them to tax the trade that would pay for the army that would build the siege engines that these castles had been designed to withstand? There was a wanton excess to this ring of Camelots circling Snowdonia. As if any dragon were ever going to come out of that lair again.

Perhaps the castles meant something else to the King. Perhaps they were precursors of the castles he thought he might one day build in the Holy Land; perhaps they were even their substitutes. Yet instead of encircling Jerusalem on behalf of Christendom, all they guarded was Dolgellau. And the towering green and slate grey of Snowdonia.

And when it came to the fate of Y Groes Gneth, Edward's actions also speak of a crusade-like quest.

While he was staying at Conway, one of Llewellyn's former clerks led a delegation to see the King. The man's name was Hugo ap Ythel and the King was so grateful to the clerk that he was given a special robe for his change in loyalty and had his university fees paid by the English state. Hugo had come to surrender Y Groes Gneth.

The presentation of Y Groes Gneth was a moment of great import for Edward. It was the symbolic climax of a perilous quest for a token of the Christ in a foreign land in which his simple soldier's faith and the righteousness of his cause had won through. In gratitude and celebration, Edward adorned Y Groes Gneth with a rich new pedestal or setting. He paraded with it to Westminster Abbey and from there to a temporary home in St Helen's Bishopgate, perhaps to acknowledge its connection to the discoverer of the True Cross. And then, ominously, portentously, he decided to keep it with him, honouring it with a place in the private chapel that travelled with him around his realm. This Welsh reliquary of the True Cross meant something to him, something personal.

In Wales, Edward had taken the cross.

7

KING EDWARD I, THE COMMUNITY OF THE REALM OF SCOTLAND AND THE BLACK ROOD

The community of the realm of Scotland had not forgotten their Wessex Queen. Successive generations honoured and treasured her Gospel Book and, a millennium later, the places that were associated with her would still be named after her. The reedy, unprepossessing strip of land where she first set foot in Scotland and met Malcolm would become known as St Margaret's Hope. The chapel named after her in Edinburgh Castle still stands; it may even have been the one she struggled to reach in the days before she died. Her descendants and countrywomen named their daughters Margaret in her honour, their sons Alexander. They treasured her remains and relics, even venerating her sark, or chemise, which was said to bring the women of the family luck in fertility and childbirth. And there was a shared consciousness among them of the holiness of her line, its propensity for piety, virginity, good works, fasting and even a reluctance for sin.

Eventually they made her a saint. Her son David's Dunfermline Abbey served as the seat of her cult; her daughter, Edith-Matilda commissioned Turgot to write her hagiography, and this and the miracle-accounts from the shrine became its sacred texts. Together they helped to form a national royal cult, equal to that of England's sainted monarch, Edward the Confessor at Westminster; and as the popularity of the cult grew, the idea of her became something like that of a guardian angel, a protectrix of Scotland.

And while Margaret and Malcolm's male line passed king-to-king down the throne of Scotland, their female line was equally assured of its destiny. Queen Edith-Matilda had a daughter, a second Matilda. And if there was anyone who exemplified the indomitable imperiousness and sense of self that passed, queen to queen, down Margaret's female line, it was Matilda.

Married to, and then widowed by, the Holy Roman Emperor, the imperially styled Empress Matilda was nominated by her father King Henry I of England to

41

be his heir, an extraordinary and radical choice given the gender arrangements of the early medieval world. She believed it too, believed she could rule alone like an empress of legend, so much so that she fought a 20-year war to assert her rights against her usurper; and although she did not become Queen in the end, her second marriage, to the Duke of Anjou, founded the Plantagenet dynasty and created the royal line of England from which Edward I and every English monarch has since been descended. In this way, Margaret and Malcolm's vision of a line of Scottish and English kings and queens came to pass, a line so connected that the idea of a united kingdom became a possibility, of two nations so equal and interlinked that they could not easily be separated.

And in the decades and centuries following its role in the deaths of Margaret and David, the Black Rood partook of this status and pulsed with a new power. It oozed not only the Holy Blood stained onto the wood of the True Cross within; it glittered not only with the prestige of the House of Wessex; but it shone also with Malcolm and Margaret's vision for Scotland: a pious, God-chosen, self-assured peer of England, the equal of any in Christendom.

* * *

It was in 1286, twelve years into Edward's reign, when Malcolm and Margaret's male-line faltered.

On 16 March 1286, just up the firth shore from St Margaret's Hope, their great-great-great-grandson, the forty-four-year-old King Alexander III was hurrying home to see his new, young wife. He was almost certainly heading for Dunfermline, and the thought of his wife in close proximity to Margaret's miraculous baby-making chemise must have spurred him on, because he lost his entourage in the dark. Unfortunately, his horse also lost its footing. It rolled him down a steep bank to his death. The place this happened is called Kinghorn, and Margaret and Malcolm's direct royal line went down with him.

Despite the urgency of his night-time ride, Alexander's queen did not prove to be a widow who had been left pregnant, and with all his children by his first wife already dead, there remained only a single hope: a two-year-old granddaughter.

She was also called Margaret, named after her famous ancestor, and the daughter of another Queen Margaret, Alexander's daughter, who had died while married to the King of Norway. After years of negotiation, which included the possibility of the toddler becoming betrothed to the heir to the throne of England, the Scottish establishment arranged for the so-called Maid of Norway to travel to Scotland via Orkney, where she too promptly died.

The political elite in Scotland was now in a quandary. There was no obvious heir, and all the minor branches of the royal house immediately saw an opportunity to stake a claim to the monarchy. The situation resulted in more than a dozen possible candidates rushing forward – a mix of illegitimate descendants, descendants of royal daughters, and even a descendant of Malcolm's brother Donald Ban, who thought it was worth pitching his coronet into the ring.

Seeing how many claimants to the throne there were from the various minor branches of the royal family, and fearing civil war, and recognising too the equilibrium of respect that had been established between the two peer kingdoms, the so-called Guardians of the Realm seem to have chosen the cousinly Plantagenet King of England to arbitrate and decide on whom the Black Rood and the other crown jewels should now be conferred.

Edward's task was simple. He had to determine which of the remaining branches of Malcolm and Margaret's dynasty had the best claim to the throne. The male claimants included Edward himself (who reserved the possibility of his own candidacy), but only two were properly credible: John Balliol, whose grandmother was David's eldest granddaughter; and Robert de Brus (the grandfather of the future king), whose grandmother was David's second eldest granddaughter.

Edward's first act in his adjudication revealed everything that Scotland needed to know. He demanded that all involved should recognise him as their over-king. Understandably, the Guardians refused, saying with reasonable sophistry that this was something that only a king could determine. Equally understandably, the main candidates conceded the point, for what hope did they have of being selected to be king otherwise?

Now he had the as-yet-unchosen king in his power, Edward also demanded possession of the royal castles and the surrender of the crown jewels, the relics, the charters and all the other symbols of the nation that touched on the royal dignity. Presumably, the Guardians thought that a temporary dispossession of both the nation's strongholds and its treasures would only serve to underline the authority of Edward's decision and so further prevent the possibility of civil war when the new king was chosen. Perhaps the Guardians felt he might not really mean to insist on his status as over-king. Perhaps the Guardians even had faith in Edward, and in the unstated but apparently mutually understood parity that had now long been established between the kingdoms. Perhaps they had no other choice.

Margaret's Black Rood had now been handed down king-to-king for over 200 years. It was probably considered a personal crown jewel, one that was kept in the possession of the king or his immediate family, and which was passed down as a royal heirloom. Like any crown jewel, it would have spoken of the continuity of the dynasty across centuries, and each king in turn would then have had to make his own accommodation with the relic. David's successors, Malcolm IV, William I, Alexander II and Alexander III, would each have had to decide where to keep it, whether within their household, in their private royal chapel, or in the safety of the treasury at Edinburgh Castle, or even in the public reverence of its namesake abbey of Holyrood. And each king would have had to determine how far to invest it with personal meaning, a meaning that was dependent not only on the extent of his personal piety, but also on the political effect that an association with the relic might have had on the community of the realm.

By the time Edward demanded it, the Black Rood seems to have been kept in the royal treasury at Edinburgh Castle. It was from here that the Guardians of Scotland handed it over for his temporary safekeeping, alongside the other crown jewels, regalia, signs and symbols of their kingdom, all given to a king who had already dispossessed the Welsh of theirs.

This transfer necessitated that the crown jewels be logged and described. In a document entitled *An Indenture of the Muniments (deeds) taken possession of in the Treasury of Edinburgh and deposited at Berwick, in the year 1291, by the Command of the English King*, the Black Rood is specifically itemised as 'a silver case covered with gold in which rests the cross which is called the Black Rood'.[4] It sounds like a smallish object, small enough to require its own silver case, almost as if it had its own jewellery box, which was itself precious.

Edward's adjudication took 18 months, but eventually, he made a decision.

The candidate John Balliol was chosen to become King John the First of Scotland. Some sort of ceremonial acknowledgement was possibly made at Berwick where the adjudication had taken place. Perhaps the Black Rood and the other crown jewels were formally handed back in preparation for the coronation ceremony that took place at Scone on St Andrew's Day 1292. But whatever the ritual around the return of the regalia, one of John's early acts as King of Scots was to do homage for Scotland to the King of England. The proud equality of Margaret's kingdom with England seemed over.

Yet despite this new public clarity about the relationship between the two kingdoms, it did not satisfy Edward. He wanted something more. The homage seems to have merely whetted his appetite for Scotland's abasement rather than blunting it. Perhaps there was something about capitulation without a conquest that he found ignoble or uninspiring; perhaps he was just jealous of the Black Rood and wanted it back.

Over the next three years, Edward made it impossible for his nominee to thrive, even as under-king. Legal disputes were used to show John the limits of his authority by allowing appeals to go up to Edward; feudal service was demanded in order to make it clear to Scotland that it could have no separate foreign policy. Eventually, the Scottish state sought desperately to protect its nationhood by allying with Edward's enemy the King of France. This was the trigger Edward needed, and his crusade for full dominion over the island of Britain entered the military phase.

Mustering his feudal host at Newcastle, Edward waited until the celebration of Easter 1296 before taking his army across the Tweed and attacking Berwick. Easily overcoming the city's ramshackle defences, the siege became a massacre in which the town's licensed Flemish merchants were burned alive as they hid in their own trade hall, while there was such a slaughter of the townsmen that the clergy begged Edward to show mercy. The ineffectual and long inexperienced Scottish feudal host was mustered in response but was easily defeated at Dunbar, and, while John fled northwards, Edinburgh was captured. A few weeks later the King was too.

Edward had made King John and now he unmade him. In a strange, vindictive pageant of humiliation, John was literally stripped of his regalia in a burlesque, anti-coronation ceremony. The un-king's sword was snapped in front of him; the royal insignia on his cloak or tabard were ripped from his back; his sword and sceptre were taken from him and presented to the English royal shrine of Edward's namesake at Westminster; and John himself was sent to the Tower of London. Only the crown could not be found. However, in a pathetic coda three years later, it reappeared in John's luggage when it was being searched prior to his banishment to France. He was trying to smuggle the crown of Scotland like so much contraband.

Having literally stripped the King, Edward now eviscerated Scotland of its royal heritage to make it an un-nation. The invasion had been so fierce and implacable that no one other than John seems to have even thought to conceal the ancient symbols of the Scottish royal state.

The Stone of Scone was snatched up from its heartland near Perth and sent to London where it would be placed under a new English coronation throne Edward had commissioned. The Black Rood was snaffled up to be added to Edward's triumphalist collection.

Yet instead of being sent to London as booty, Edward kept the Black Rood for himself. it meant something to him, something personal. He hung it alongside Y Groes Gneth in his mobile military chapel so it could be with him wherever he went. Perhaps he even placed it round his neck.

It was as if Edward was collecting the totems of the nations he ruled and taking their symbolic power to himself. He was stealing the splinters of the Holy Tree that were kept in his lands and bringing them together, surrounding himself with their combined ethereal power. And he used their power to humiliate and compel. As he progressed his conquest of Scotland, he made those Scottish magnates who capitulated swear their loyalty to him over the two captured national crosses, the

Black Rood and Y Groes Gneth. When he reached Elgin, the northern most point of the invasion, he obliged the fleeing former Guardian of the Realm and stalwart of the national cause Bishop Wishart to swear loyalty over the Black Rood. It was an act that suggests that in Edward's mind at least it had some public significance, that is still represented Scotland in the same way that Y Groes Gneth represented Wales, that it was not just a private relic of the royal family.[5]

For Edward this was enough – the victories, the symbolic disinvestment, the swearing of oaths of loyalty over his collection of holy national talismans. For him, this would be enough for Scotland to understand its place in his scheme of the realm. But for Scotland, it was not the end. Over the coming years, Edward was forced to return again and again as Scotland rallied and then rallied again in the name of the exiled King John. Edward's first easy victory of 1296 belied the years of grinding effort a real conquest of Scotland would take; but, with glacial implacability driven by Edward's will, the more powerful English state gained slow momentum. Flashes of Scottish success – at Stirling Bridge under William Wallace, and at Roslin – illuminated the possibility of another outcome, and without Edward's driving certainty, it is probable that all the rest of England would have given up. But Edward was driven by a vision that was other-worldly in its intensity.

In 1299, in the middle of this long campaign of subjugation, Edward married for a second time. His beloved first wife Eleanor – she who had sucked poison from an assassin's wound during his only real crusade – had died in 1290, and with characteristic monumentalism Edward had arranged for the stages of her body's final journey to be marked out with a series of high stone crosses that picked out the route down to London from the abbey where she had died. With the same disproportionate élan of his Welsh castles, Edward had marked up on his country the last journey the still corporeal body of his beloved had taken in the world.

Edward's second wedding seems to have been marked with the same grandiosity and vision. A garbled account of the marriage feast survives. Although misattributed to his first wedding, it suggests again that Edward saw his conquest of Britain in mythic, Arthurian terms. According to the muddled source, a Dutch chronicler, Edward held another round table as part of the festivities. This featured a knightly tournament and an Arthurian themed feast which included a role-play in which squires from Wales and 'Irlant', and a Loathly Damsel from 'Cornuaelge' burst in between the courses like the Green Knight to demand that Edward's court avenge the wrongs they had suffered in the lands from which they had fled.

Allowing that the Dutch chronicler seems to have confused the first marriage with the second, Ireland with Scotland, and Cornuaelge with Cornwall or

Kenilworth – a castle Edward had captured during the Baron's War some 30 years before – we can glimpse a celebration in which the legends of Arthur and the military achievements of Edward were interlaced. Edward of course would have been playing Arthur.

Over the next few years, the grinding conquest of Scotland reached a grudging conclusion. A catastrophic French defeat in 1302 made a French-backed return for King John unlikely, an outcome that a new peace treaty between France and England turned into an impossibility. Without the prospect of regaining a king of their own, the majority of Scottish magnates realised they had no choice but to accept the English one. All Edward needed was a final spectacular.

By April 1304, only the castle at Stirling still held out. Edward gathered what, following a parliament in St Andrews, were now effectively an Anglo-Scottish force for a final showdown. He even built a construction with an oriel window so his new queen could watch the entertainment. The castle had Greek fire hurled at it and endured bombardment from all the siege engines in Scotland, yet still it held out. Edward called up a fresh monster – a new contraption called War Wolf – and although the garrison had already offered unconditional surrender, Edward refused to let anyone leave until the War Wolf had been tried out.

The next year, the die-hard fugitive Wallace was captured and sent in chains to London for vicious execution. Edward's attempt to conquer Scotland was over.

Edward now had it all. He was the namesake of King Edward the Confessor; he was the heir to King Arthur, whose bones he had viewed to show the Welsh that their once-king would not be a future king; his son and future heir-apparents would revel in the stolen title Prince of Wales for ever after; he was King of Scots and had gifted the Scots king-making stone to the shrine of Edward the Confessor to show the Scots that all their kings would now be English; the holy knights of his revived round table could drink from a grail made from the seal-matrices of Wales; in a fulfilment of the prophecy of Merlin, where the three thrones of the island of Britain were brought together into one citadel, the splintered fragments of the holy tree had been brought together in his chapel. He held the ancient Black Rood and the mysterious Croes Gneth close by him, as the final most personal emblems of his divine approbation to rule Scotland and Wales.

In November 1304, as he had done during the campaign, Edward made personal oblations to Y Groes Gneth and the Black Rood in his private chapel, paying thanks for the victory.[6] The world was in order at last. He was confirmed King of all Britain, and as king he possessed the totems of the lands he ruled, and as a Christian king these totems were of Christ. This flattered Edward's soldier's sense of symbolism. All was right with the world, in good battle order.

* * *

In March 1306, exactly ten years after Edward first crossed the Tweed to besiege Berwick, Robert Bruce, the grandson of the candidate for the kingship, was proclaimed the rightful King of Scots in a rebel ceremony at Scone.

It was a great gathering 'attended and consented to', says an English source, 'by four bishops, five earls and the people of the country'. An unknown craftsman fashioned a new crown, a circlet of gold, for the rebel king to wear; Bishop Wishart fetched out some royal robes that he had kept hidden for just such a hoped-for moment; the Countess of Buchan, the aunt of the Earl of Fife represented her nephew in his hereditary king-making role in the ceremony; and, although there was no longer any Stone of Scone, no one, not even Edward, could quarry away all the earth magic from the ancient place of enthronement. The community of the realm conferred the kingship on Robert Bruce by assent, making him their new King of Scots.

Edward I, his health failing, gathered his forces and sent them once more towards Scotland. The new King Robert fled north on foot, becoming a guerrilla fighter and vanishing into the Highlands or islands for four and a half months. His womenfolk took the horses and tried to make for the coast and Norway, but were overtaken and captured. Edward, shockingly and in the Italian style, had the Bruce women imprisoned in wooden cages which were placed on the tops of turrets open to the elements. The Countess of Buchan's cage was shaped like a crown in grim ridicule for her role in the coronation. Such was Edward's wrath, when one of the five earls who graced the ceremony was captured, he was killed with the full torture of the traitor. It was the first execution of an earl in England for more than 200 years.

In 1307, Edward was once more making for Scotland with a massive army when his health began to deteriorate further. He was being carried north on a litter in his last act of fury when he faltered at a place called Burgh on Sands, on the flat estuary land of Cumbria, in a reedy British amphitheatre ringed by the distant mountains of Snowdonia, of southern Scotland and of northern England. Here Edward I died. And like his great-great-great-great grandmother Margaret and his great-great-great-great-uncle David, the Black Rood was near him.

'In a casket marked with the sign of the cross...' the royal clerks recorded in his private chapel, 'la Blakrood of Scotland of gold-work with a gold chain, in a wooden case with a silver gilt exterior.'[7]

But if, like his forebears Margaret and David, he called for the Black Rood in his final moments, it was not recorded.

8

KINGS EDWARD II AND EDWARD III, Y GROES GNETH AND THE BLACK ROOD

> And when the New Year was come, on that day the
> nobles on the dais were double served, when the
> king came with his knights into the great hall and
> the chanting in the chapel was ended. And clerks
> and others set up a loud cry, and they kept the Feast
> of Christmas anew, and they gave and received New
> Year's gifts, and much talking was there about the gifts.
>
> *Sir Gawain and the Green Knight*
> (translated by Earnest J. B. Kirtlan)

The loss of the Black Rood did nothing to hinder Scotland.

Following Edward's death and, lacking the impetus of his will, the English were driven out of the country. During the reign of Edward's son, a second Edward, the Scots surged from strength to strength. They hurled the new English King out of the country, annihilating his army and forcing him to run for his life and liberty from a stream near Stirling called the Bannock burn. Hounded as he fled, his horse killed beneath him, Edward II had to abandon his shield and even his privy seal in his desperate haste and humiliation.

After this catastrophe, his fractious court seems not to have been able to bring itself to acknowledge the Black Rood again, and it enters a period of obscurity in which its status and whereabouts can only be speculated on. For after Banockburn and the triumph of King Robert Bruce, who in England would want to acknowledge this mystical talisman of Scotland? Instead of being a trophy symbolising England's divinely approved destiny to rule the all the lands of Britain, the Black Rood would have become a hollow haunting symbol of defeat, a shameful *memento mori* of everything the father had been and everything the son was not. It must have taunted the new King at every turn.

Y Groes Gneth in contrast retained its symbolic potency. Wales remained conquered. The Welsh reliquary was kept in the King's Chapel of the Tower of London, and it was present at one of the most significant moments of Edward II's reign, the attempt by the barons and nobles, alongside Edward's French queen and her family, to save the King from himself by banishing his disruptive and insufferable favourite, Piers Gaveston. Y Groes Gneth was used in 1308 and 1311 to extract oaths of contrition and good future intent from Gaveston, the man they held to be responsible for the failings of the reign.

But this unlucky King, who had first lost Scotland, eventually lost England too. In a *coup d'etat* led by his humiliated queen and her avaricious lover, the King was arrested, deposed, imprisoned and perhaps even murdered. His estranged teenage son, a third Edward, was placed on the throne in 1327 to be ruled by his mother.

It was to his namesake grandfather that the new King Edward III looked for inspiration. His father's stature had been eviscerated; his mother and her lover seemed only interested in gathering to themselves the riches of the kingdom. The fourteen-year-old therefore had nowhere else to turn for a vision of kingship but to the memory of his hero grandfather and to their shared inspiration in King Arthur. At the boy's coronation in Westminster Abbey, the grandfather's tomb had been draped in cloth of gold to mark his mighty influence and enduring presence. The English crown – the so-called crown of Saint Edward – was gently lowered on to the boy's head, with extra layers of padding provided to hold it there. Even so, it was said, the coronating bishops refused to risk letting go of the crown. They had to support the teetering headwear in its place.

For several years, the boy-king was ruled by his mother and her lover, and it was during this minority that two diplomatic undertakings were entered into on his behalf, the ramifications of which would dominate his reign after he came of age.

The first was a peace treaty with Scotland. In gleeful contempt for Edward III's coronation, the Scots immediately raided the north of England. In response, and perhaps in order to mark some fresh resolve, Edward III followed his grandfather and father north to be the nominal lead of an English army sent to punish their impertinence. Playing cat-and-mouse through Durham and the borders, the Scots outmanoeuvred the English. The two armies ended up in a stand-off across the upper valley of the River Wear, with the Scots occupying the high southern banks. Caught out by a night attack in which a raiding party forded the river and penetrated the English camp to within reach of the King's pavilion, the English woke to find the Scots army vanished. Such was his inability to live out his dreams and dominate the Scots, even on his own hillside, that the boy-king of England was said to have burst into frustrated tears.

It was in this context – with the Scots able to raid the north of England with impunity, attacking its castles and even appearing to contemplate the annexation of Northumberland – that the queen-mother and her lover agreed to a peace treaty that gave the dying Robert Bruce everything he had ever wanted. It was a capitulation so complete that it could hardly have been imagined or wished for at the outset. The borders were to return to those of 1286, to include the great revenue-creating port of Berwick; the King of Scots was to be acknowledged as an equal to the King of England; and in recognition of this equality, Edward III's sister was to be married to King Robert's infant son, David. Finally, the Stone of Scone and the other signs and symbols including it seems the Black Rood were offered up for surrender and repatriation.[8]

The final endorsement of his life's work came just as King Robert's ambassador won for his heir David the thing that every Scots king had wanted since the balking of David I at his inauguration two centuries before: the right granted by the pope to be crowned and anointed by bishops, just like any other king of Christendom, answerable only to God.

The end of King Robert's life therefore saw a re-commitment and re-exposition of everything Margaret, Malcolm and their descendants had striven for. The settlement with England reached back to their founding vision, complete equality with, and in some ways even superiority over, England. The treaty took both countries back to the time before Edward I, when there had been peaceful parity and equilibrium between the kingdoms. It rewrote Edward I's 1292 arbitration between the Bruce and Balliol claims to the throne, showing the world how wrong Edward's original judgement had been, confirming that God had looked on the vicious thirty-year war of independence, weighed in on the hundreds of thousands of individual trials-by-combat on every battlefield, and shown that it was the Bruce dynasty that was favoured, that it was the Bruce claim that a wise, pious arbitrator should have chosen. The peace treaty wrote Edward I out of history. It was as if the attempted subjugation of Scotland had never happened. It was as if he had not existed.

The English court might have accepted the expediency of this, but it was too much for some of their countrymen and women. They could not control Scotland. They could not control the decisions being made by the regency government in its peace-making; but they could show their disapproval through the symbols they had to hand. At the prospect that the Stone of Scone and the other symbols would be returned, the Londoners rioted and would not allow the Stone's removal from Westminster. They would not accept the disrespect it did to the memory of Edward I and to his abbey's namesake saint, Edward the Confessor. It is also very unlikely the Black Rood was ever returned.

Despite the non-return of the Stone of Scone, the coronation and anointing of King David II of Scotland went ahead on 24 November 1331. The country had waited an oddly long time – two and a half years following King Robert's death – to inaugurate the new King. The delay could have been caused by the officiates waiting on the return of the Stone; or the officiates could have been waiting on detailed instructions from Rome – for no bishop in Scotland had ever performed a crown-and-oil ceremony before; or they may just have been waiting for the infant David to grow sufficiently to be able to perform his part in the ritual with some reliability. Swaddled in cloth of gold, the now seven-year-old David and his 10-year-old bride were duly anointed and then crowned with coronets that had been specially made to fit their little heads, while a tiny sceptre was placed in the King's little hand, like a game of cup and ball.

It must have been one of the most moving ceremonies ever to take place at Scone: the boy-king of Scots and his English princess bride; the two countries equal at last; the haloing, sacring-oil moistening the monarch's little skull and dripping onto the bedrock of Scotland for the first time; the heavens sanctifying the pagan stone; yet the future of the Bruce dynasty so insecure; the wedded children so vulnerable; their union unconsummatable. It was all too much for David II. The English said he soiled himself in his nervousness.

The second diplomatic undertaking that the teenage King Edward III gave which he would come to retract was when, at the age of 16, he performed homage to the new King of France. Edward III had a strong claim to the French throne. His mother was sister to the former king and, as his uncle the King had died with no male heir, Edward was in line for the succession. Nevertheless, France refused to accept inheritance down the female line, and on 6 June 1329 Edward III accepted France's decision and paid homage to the new King in the cathedral of Amiens for the lands he held in the country. This moment of adolescent capitulation, repeated almost in secret and shame two year later was, together with the Treaty of Edinburgh, was to define much of the rest of Edward's life.

Born at Windsor Castle, the new boy-king of England was fascinated by history, chivalry and adventure. In the royal cabinet of curiosities there, he would have been able to wonder at the knife that had been used in the attempted assassination of his grandfather fifty years before – the one that had caused the wound from which his grandmother Eleanor had sucked the poison – and perhaps it was the contemplation of this exciting relic of a crusade that triggered Edward's lifelong ancestor-worship of his grandfather.

However, while he emulated Edward I, his was not an attempted reincarnation. Edward I had been remote, monumental and autocratic. The old king's architectural legacy – the Welsh castles, the Eleanor crosses, and his violent sculpting of a new kingdom of Britain from the lands of Scotland and Wales – were emanations of a single-minded intensity married to a stolid symbolism.

The grandson was more personable, egalitarian and lighter of touch, and more sensitive to the profound. He loved knightly camaraderie, relished participating as an equal in bands of brothers with a common knightly cause, sometimes even taking part incognito in tournaments as just another knight; he thrilled to the panache and risk-taking bravado of troupes of men, often drawing together his supporters to act like lightening against his enemies. He had great bonhomie, was at his ease with ordinary people, and he enjoyed the softer symbolism and panoply of monarch: the pageants, tournaments and royal hunts; the ostentatious liveries, colourful robes and heraldic devices; the honours he could bestow; the theatres of ritual, spectacle and revelation. His eventual founding of the knightly Order of the Garter speaks to this sense of chivalric community, knightly *egalite* and theatricalism.

But he was no less ambitious than his grandfather, for his kingship or his kingdom. At the age of 17, he threw aside the regency of his mother and her lover and assumed the full rights of a king. Immediately, he repudiated the Treaty of Edinburgh that had written his grandfather's life's work out of history, and he deliberately re-established his grandfather's policy towards Scotland, even supporting a private initiative by the son of Edward I's failed puppet John Balliol to regain the throne of Scotland. And it was the initial success of this venture and successive English incursions that drove the Bruce areas of control back into the Highlands and caused the newly crowned and anointed David II to flee Scotland and spend his adolescence in exile in France.

It was also to France that the attention of Edward would eventually turn. The mystical Arthurian apocrypha, the Prophesies of Merlin, claimed that Arthur had first united the lands of Britain, and then brought Britain and Gaul into a single realm, before going on towards Jerusalem and to recapture the holy city. What greater ambition could the grandson of Edward I have? If the grandfather had brought the Welsh and Scottish pieces of the True Cross together, the grandson would fulfil the promise of Merlin and go on to capture Gaul and dominate Christendom by restoring Jerusalem.

Having established his own strength and rebuilt his kingdom, it was in 1340, after thirteen years of his reign, that Edward announced his magnificent, astonishing project. He proclaimed himself King of France: a dream-like, almost adolescent vision that combined Arthurian mysticism, knightly derring-do and chivalric ambition of the highest order.

The first significant moment in the campaign to make this dream true was a naval encounter between a small English fleet and a much larger French force of ships and men in the battle of Sluys. The English may have been inferior in numbers but they had far superior archers and archery tactics, and they annihilated the French. In holy gratitude, and with his own theatrical panache, Edward ordered five ornamental ships to be made of gold and presented to various major religious houses in memorial to the victory.

Less effectual forays on land into Flanders and Brittany followed, but, by the spring of 1345, Edward had the finances and political support in place to attempt the next impossible stage – a full invasion of France using the largest English army to go overseas. A storm prevented the first planned invasion in the summer of 1345 and the army had to disband over the winter, but by 1346, everything was in place. England would invade France

And it was at the beginning of 1346, a year in which Edward III and all of England and Europe knew would be his year of destiny, that Edward rescued the Black Rood from its obscurity. He asked for it to be brought to him from the treasury of Westminster in order that it should be kept by his side.

At the beginning of a new year, on the day after Epiphany, at the culmination of the medieval Christmas and of the courtly festivities for which he was famed, Edward honoured the memory and habit of his grandfather by keeping faith with the Black Rood and keeping it near him during his greatest adventure – the campaign to secure the kingship of France.

Until that strange Christmas happening, the Black Rood seems to have languished unregarded and dishonoured in the English treasury where it had lain since the embarrassing reign of Edward II. In contrast, its Welsh cousin, Y Groes Gneth had remained at the centre of royal ritual. Not only had it played its central part in the calamitous reign of Edward II, it was also the relic used to bless the Maundy money distributed by the King. Edward III seems to have enhanced it with new jewels and had it kept near him so he could make personal oblations to it, just like his grandfather.

But while it has been argued that Edward might have requested the Black Rood so he could offer it as a bribe to Scotland, this seems unlike him. Certainly, by taking such a large army overseas Edward was risking an attack from Scotland; indeed for the now-returned, now-adult and French-raised David II, his alliance with France made some kind of military support a political and personal obligation. It is therefore just possible that the Black Rood was ordered up to be gifted back to Scotland as a placating peace offering. But, given Edward's ambitions in France and Scotland, and his regard for his grandfather, it seems unlikely.

Instead, right at the beginning of his most audacious year, as the Christmas season ended and the new-year gifts were made, Edward returned to the favoured relic of his grandfather, the one that was near him at his death, and re-appropriated it, making the Black Rood a present to himself.[9]

9

THE BATTLES OF 1346

Edward's army embarked for France in July and made landfall in Normandy. Edward's eldest son, Edward Prince of Wales, who was to become known as the Black Prince, was sixteen. The invasion was his entry into manhood; he was knighted when they landed. The army was divided into three sections, or battles. The first, the vanguard, was given to the Black Prince. The second, the centre, was commanded by the King. While the rear-guard was entrusted, unusually, to a bishop: the new Bishop of Durham, Thomas Hatfield.

Hatfield was in his mid-thirties. He had been a clerk of the King and had come to prominence during the rebuilding of Stirling and Bothwell castles in the Scottish campaigns. He had then risen through the administrative ranks to become Edward's Receiver of the Chamber – an important position in the executive. He had recently been elevated to the position of Bishop of Durham, presumably in order to provide strong leadership to the north of England in its defence against Scotland. The French campaign was, however, too exciting to resist, and Hatfield's concession to his new episcopal position may only have involved the commissioning of a new suit of armour, with a helmet that featured a plumed mitre – a bishop's head-dress – on its crest. Hatfield brought with him a substantial retinue of three bannerets, forty-eight knights, 162 esquires and eighty-one archers. He may also have been armed with a mace, as bishops were not supposed to draw blood.

From its landfall, Edward's army advanced on a front twenty miles wide, devastating the fields and villages in its path and sacking the city of Caen in an attempt to provoke the French to respond. Reaching the Seine on 7 August, the English marched upriver on its western banks searching for a place to cross into France proper; they were shadowed on the other bank by a French army who busied themselves either breaking or fortifying the bridges they came to in order to prevent the incursion. In this manner, the English arrived in Poissy on 13 August and here Edward paused to honour his maternal grandfather the former King of France, whose heart was buried in the church he had founded. Crossing the river at this point, they were now only fifteen miles from Paris. This galvanised the French into action and the two kings exchanged ultimata – each inviting the other to give battle. Edward then moved his army away north, towards the River Somme, presumably to link up with a force bringing new supplies to the port of Crotoy, and for a moment it looked like a rapid French countermove might have trapped the English between the river and the sea. It was only a daring overnight crossing to the north bank of the river that gave the English the freedom of manoeuvre and the cover they needed in the forest around the village of Crécy.

It was here that the vastly superior French force decided to give battle. Despite the English occupying a strongly defensible position, the French magnates were so confident of their victory that they started to discuss which English prisoners each would be able to capture and ransom. In reaction to this nonchalance, the King of France ordered the unfurling of his own great totem, the Oriflamme, a sacred scarlet banner dyed, it was said, with the blood of Saint Denis. Its unfurling signified that the French would take no prisoners, that this would be a fight to the death. As one English chronicler wrote, 'It was called the Oriflamme to imply that the mercy of the French was entirely consumed, and no one's life could be spared, just as flaming oil destroys everything that can be burnt'.

Such was the eagerness of the French to engage the smaller English army that they would not wait until the next morning to rest their men and horses. Attacking towards sunset, their mounted knights in their eagerness trampled over their own Genoese crossbow men who were retreating under an onslaught of arrows by the English longbow men. Crushing the shrieking Genoese beneath them, the French knights arrived at the English lines where they discovered the strength of the defensive tactics that the English had learned from, and then practised on, the Scots. The slope of the ground slowed their momentum; pitted holes a foot deep and a foot wide dug in front of the English lines broke the legs of their horses; arrows rained down from the longbow men on each flank, catching them in a maelstrom of crossfire and killing and wounding their unarmoured mounts; explosive projectiles used in battle for the first time by the English terrified the horses further. Manoeuvre became increasingly difficult in the press, with some French knights simply being crushed to death. Somehow the English seemed to have used the terrain and their positioning to restrict the field of battle to a small area where, an eyewitness claimed, 1,500 French knights and squires were killed.

Heroically, famously, the teenage Black Prince was in the thick of the action, bearing the brunt of the waves of French attacks and at one point almost being overcome. An appeal to his father was sent to the rear where the king was safely ensconced on the high ground by a windmill. Supposedly, epically, chivalrously, Edward met the appeal with the words 'Let the boy win his spurs'.

It was not far from a massacre. In the end, according to a French prisoner 'the flower of the whole knighthood of France had been killed'. The French standard bearer died within sight of his King and the terrifying Oriflamme was found the next day, torn and abandoned on the ground. The body of France's ally, the blind King John of Bohemia, was found with his men, their horses roped together. All had been killed as one unit as they led him shoulder to shoulder into the battle. Bishop Hatfield officiated at his funeral.

'That evening, having found the King of Bohemia's body', wrote an eye-witness, 'they had it washed in warm water, wrapped in clean linen and placed in a horse litter. The bishop of Durham and the clergy who were there celebrated the solemn rites for the dead in the presence of the King and his companions'.

Despite this victory, the King and his army pressed on northwards to attack Calais. The city would take a year to fall, and it was probably here, during the long autumn siege, that Bishop Hatfield received a letter from John Fossor, who held the office of Prior at Durham Cathedral, bringing the news that those aboard had dreaded: an invasion of northern England by Scotland.

'Although we suppose that various letters have been sent by a great many people to your reverence about these deeds done by the cruel race of Scots in English lands... we bring news in these letters for your lordship to hear', wrote the Prior.

'Shortly after the feast of the archangel St Michael, the aforesaid Scots, in a state of complete excitement, and with a multitude of men-at-arms and foot soldiers – who, just as we heard afterwards from several of them, did not believe that all the people of both France and England could resist them, even if their men had been greatly inflamed together – invading the country of England, they cruelly ravaged all the lands through which they passed with fire and murderous swords, with scant regard for age or sex; and among these evil deed, which they atrociously committed, they captured the fortress of Liddel, which was held by Walter de Selby, and killed whomsoever they found within it. Afterwards, however, as the Scots passed by another fortress, called Haydenhall near Corbridge, it was surrendered to them, to save the lives of the inhabitants'.

'Next, continuing for a day's journey, on a fine October day around nine, they came near Durham City, showing themselves upon the moor of Bearpark, by arranging their battle lines, as if all ready to fight. But then, without further ado, leaving the moor, they wheeled around toward our manor of Bearpark, and spent the whole night within the park, not one of them remaining outside, just as we know with certainty'.

Bishop Hatfield may not yet have known Bearpark. The priory manor-house lay on the top of a strange promontory that stretched along the middle of a wide valley just to the west of Durham. This spur of land, with its views to the mountains of the west, was one of the largest parks in England. Originally named Beau Repair – beautiful recuperation – the priory and its surrounds were a retreat for the Durham monks.

Yet despite the pastoral setting and view, Bearpark was an odd, disconcerting place. A mile-long tongue of land extending the wrong way into the valley, the spur was more or less moated on three sides: to the north by the deep, dry, dammed valley of the Browney, filled with marsh and remnant oxbow lakes, and to the west and the south by precipitous clay cliffs that had been formed by the river when, millennia before, it had driven a new route south to meet the Weir. It was a strange, vulnerable promontory, with a single, level track in and out, and it was here that they spent the night, their tents and pavilions 'of the richest and noblest sort, the like of which had not been seen in these parts for a long time'. But despite the strangeness, they could sleep safely with no concern that this beautiful, relaxing park was a trap. Northern England, with no fighting men left in the county, was there for the taking. Or so the King believed.

King David II was no longer the incontinent child of his anointing. Now 22, he was, as the Scottish poet of the campaign put it 'young, stout and well made, and yearned for to see fighting'.

This was his opportunity for family revenge. His ravaging of the land 'with fire and murderous swords' and his killing of captives 'with scant regard for age or sex' was no different to Edward III's riotous, provoking progress through France. But David's motivation was not the same. Before he had been born, the English had left his aunt to suffer in a cage hanging in the open air, sent his stepsister to a nunnery and imprisoned his mother for eight years. Now was the time for the viciousness with which King Edward I had treated Scotland and the Bruce family to be repaid.

Even the Scottish poet was shocked by David's style of revenge.

> *Excepting children and women*
> *Without mercy they slew them*
> *They slew them all too cruelly*

The Scots and their mercenaries had been in England fourteen days already when they arrived at Bearpark. The display on the hilltop above Durham, the formation into three squadrons with banners flying, would have demonstrated their strength, their discipline and their willingness to attack the walled cathedral city which lay ungarrisoned a few hundred yards below them. The display was designed to intimidate and bring the Durham monks out to parlay, to pay a ransom and provide the Scots with the provisions they needed to advance further into England and which may have been running low.

By now, David would have had booty and victory enough to confirm his power. He could have returned to Scotland with his head high and his debts to France and his family repaid, and indeed, one of his commanders Sir William de Douglas is said to have advised him to turn back. David would not be deflected, however. He did not believe there were sufficient fighting men in England to oppose him. He is recorded as saying: 'There are none in England but wretched monks, disreputable priests, swineherds, cobblers, and skinners; they dare not face me, I am safe enough'.

Of course, the further south he went, he knew it would become more likely that he would encounter some form of opposition, but it was unimaginable that anything would happen so far north. So he stayed the night in Bearpark to see what effect his presence and malign intent would have on the monks below.

The King, they claim, was troubled by bad dreams.

At dawn the next morning, the landscape was covered in mist. The unfamiliar fields and dykes were rendered all the more alien as the army began to wake and the surroundings of Bearpark slowly formed themselves out of the grey-white haze. It was the beginning of autumn, the land newly ploughed and sown, the trees turning, the first leaf-fall settling on the ground. The hedges were filled with rose hips, toadstools, Michaelmas daisies and windblown thistle-heads. The brier leaves and bracken fronds were turning orange at the tips, and acorns were lying green and umber on the rich black earth.

Sometime that morning, as the King's household was preparing breakfast, there was a sudden unexpected disturbance at the edge of the camp.

Shouting hotly, 'like a man enraged', his commander Sir William de Douglas and what remained of an early-morning 500-man raiding party sped through the tents and pavilions to reach the King.

'David, rise quickly', Sir William shouted, 'look, all the English are attacking us'.

Breathlessly, Sir William told, how only a few miles to the south, an English army had materialised out of the fog before him, how he had heard but not seen the clamour and clanking of thousands of men, horses and weaponry, and how, not knowing which way to turn, the two forces had stumbled upon each other in the haze, A running battle had ensued in which 300 of the Scots contingent had been killed.

At first, David will not believe Sir William, but he is assured in the strongest terms.

'Oh feared King', Sir William is said to have exclaimed, 'saving your peace, you will find otherwise. There are many valiant men coming swiftly upon us, and they want to fight'.

A moment of profound shock must have descended on the camp as everyone strained to hear what had happened.

'Our host then all afraid was', comments the Scottish poet, and then the camp was thrown into sudden confusion, even panic, as the soldiery understood the situation, exposed on this cliff and bog-rimmed peninsular, with an English reserve army bearing down on them from only a mile or two away.

David calmly, or affecting calm, ordered breakfast, then his mount and his standard. But, as the realisation of what is about to happen crept in to him, he became excited and even joyous that the battle he had wanted is near. He took his standard and embellished it somehow, 'pompously' says an English account, all of the time 'ritually and repeatedly affirming himself "King of the Scots without any obstruction"'.

With gifted timing, it was then that two Durham monks were brought before the King. Chastened by the calm display of battle readiness the afternoon before, they had been drawn out to parlay, presumably to offer a ransom to save their city. It was not the ideal moment.

'Behold, these false monks speak with me craftily', David is recorded as saying, 'for they detain us here in conference so that the English army might attack us suddenly while we are thus deceived'. He ordered the two monks beheaded, but in the confusion of that morning they were forgotten and managed to slip away.

Mounting his warhorse, David announced he would return for his breakfast when he has killed all the English. He ordered his commanders to form his army into the three battles and marched them off the promontory of Bearpark and towards the Neville's Cross, a way marker on the old Roman road that crested the hill outside Durham. It was said his breakfast was left unattended and dropped into the fire.

Somewhere on the moor, between Bearpark, the Neville's Cross and the slopes of the Red Hills which career precipitously down to the edge of the City, the two armies sighted each other for the first time. According to one report, those in the first rank of the Scots army were 'raging together with unrestrained fury against the English, surging forward, unwilling to stop, confident in their own strength'. In response, the English prayed and turned towards the Scots 'in good spirits'.

From morning to early afternoon, they stayed like this, the two armies staring each other out, their banners flying, as the sun climbed up behind the English lines.

The first engagement seems to have been an archery barrage from the English flanks at around the middle of the afternoon. This forced the Scots to change position. And in response, a Scots knight, Sir John Graham, tried to gather together 100 mounted lancers to break up the English archers, but when no one would volunteer, he charged them alone, his warhorse killed beneath him.

The front rank of the Scots adopted hoplite steadfastness under the onslaught of arrows.

'The Scots did not flee, and with heads bent and covered in iron, densely drawn against the English attack, with helmets polished and shields fastened precisely, they withstood the arrows of the English at the beginning of the battle...' And when they counter-attacked, they pushed the English back a number of times. 'Twice our archers and soldiers retreated, but our men-at-arms stood firm and fought stubbornly until the archers and foot soldiers reassembled'.

Although the location is not certain, the landscape seems to have played a decisive part. The steep banks and drainage ditches on the plateau between the steep Redhills and the precipitous Browney valley made tactical manoeuvring difficult and the Scots particularly seem to have been the most affected. Like their French allies at Crécy, a sense of their being packed-in pervades the accounts of the battle: '...the first line of armed men was greeted with fatal blows', says one chronicler. 'The warriors on each side stood more prepared for death than flight. You could see the Scots wearied from exertion, so terrified by the blows from axe heads, yet standing, so that where perhaps there stood ten, each supporting the others, the felling of one with one blow, meant felling of all together; just as those who saw them slaughtered fell back'.

Penned in by earth cliffs, dykes and steep slopes, the Scots found themselves in a 'right annoyous place where none without hurt might lift a hand'.

The men and commander at the Scots rear, seeing their better armed, better drilled countrymen becoming outflanked and hemmed in by the English, began to sense that the battle would be lost and so started to retreat and run, with some of the foot soldiers said to have stolen their lords' horses.

The English chronicle is scathing about the rearguard commander's decision, for it appears he took flight 'without giving or receiving a blow from sword or lance'. He would be 'better called "Earl Absent" in his homeland' sneers another, 'for he came late, but did very well, always standing far off... and not wishing to see the end of the affair. In this conflict he harmed no one... overwhelmed by cowardice... fled valiantly'.

Despite their certainty that the battle was about to be lost, when the rearguard had made two miles, they looked back into the low sun and saw the banners of the Scots still flying, surrounded by the banners of the English.

It was here that the press was at its most concentrated. In the melee, an ambitious, ruthless and probably psychopathic English squire called John de Coupland began to fight his way towards David, who was 'ensnared with his men between ditches'. To capture a king for ransom would be as great a prize as any booty, and driven by this ambition de Coupland 'delivered such blows among the foe that it is said those who felt his hefty clouts were able to fight no longer'.

The Scots nobility and men at arms circled themselves around the King to protect him 'like a round tower' but, assaulted by arrows and eventually surrounded, this praetorian guard was picked off one by one until there were barely forty left.

De Copeland now fought his way closer until he found himself in the face of the King. David, who had already taken two arrows in his face, fought ferociously, knocking out two of de Copeland's teeth with his gauntleted fist, but now the end was inevitable. The King was captured, the battle over, and the fleeing Scots were massacred with glee.

At that time of the year, the mist at dusk seeps low out of the ground like the souls of the dead. And darkness could not have come too soon for the fleeing Scots.

* * *

'At that hour, to the greater joy of the people of the English Church', concluded Prior Fosser's letter to Bishop Hatfield, 'both sides fought strenuously, bitterly and very fiercely. However, God Almighty, in Whose hands lay the cords of the kingdom, and, just as He pleases Himself, wounds and heals, humbles and exalts, He provided the English with a miraculous victory over the Scots, restoring to those inhabitants of the northern parts, whom the Scots long oppressed, the joy of freedom for which they had yearned'.

'In this conflict, David, who called himself King of the Scots, was captured, gravely wounded by an arrow in the face; indeed many valiant men of Scotland were slain and lay strew about over the moor of Bearpark, miserably exposed, the names and number of whom I certainly need not recount to you; in any event, you will have them related sufficiently by others. Nonetheless, many were captured, of whom one, though not valiant, is nonetheless renowned for his malice, William Douglas; his name and others are enclosed in the document presented to you. Few of us in the same battle were killed'.

10

King Edward III and Y Groes Gneth at Windsor and the Black Rood at Durham

The victories in the battles of Crécy and Neville's Cross established for Edward and England a continental fame and status that the King and country had not experienced except in the tales of King Arthur. The capture of the King of Scots, and the capture of the King of France that followed, the destruction of the Scottish and French nobility and their armies, the seizure of Calais, all were achievements that took the realm of England into an epic new European league of greatness and ambition. In gratitude, Edward III returned in triumph and held a series of lavish celebrations. A brilliant sequence of rapturous tournaments in the summer and autumn of 1347 climaxed in the inception of the Order of the Garter at Windsor Castle the following year. Made up of the King, the Prince of Wales and twenty-four companion knights, the Order was to institutionalise everything that was dear to the king and his court. It was to be Arthurian, chivalric, egalitarian, erotic, convivial, theatrical, masculine and very ostentatious. Windsor was Edward's favourite castle, it was where he had been born and was said to have been founded by Arthur himself. Where could be better to re-create the legendary King's round table of pious knights than at this new Camelot?

And to ground the Order in faith and to convey the profundity of its Christian vision and the seriousness of his commitment, Edward determined to bequeath one of his most cherished and symbolic relics to the Order, both to honour its foundation and to serve as its celebrated centrepiece.

The Black Rood would surely have been considered for this honour. If it had indeed been kept close to the King during his invasion of France, it would already have done much to have restored its reputation as a paladin of a rightful king and of the success of a God-chosen nation.

Yet the Black Rood would always have an element of ambiguity about its powers. For all that the King of Scots had been humiliatingly captured, it was evident from the cousinly way that Edward was hosting the arrow-pocked David that he was not to be considered an illegitimate usurper, but instead was to be regarded as a peer and as an anointed king. Indeed, these two former child-kings of England and Scotland, one who had cried in his first battle, the other who had wet himself on the coronation throne, were becoming something like friends.

Whatever their personal relationship however, Scotland itself remained unconquered. While you could build a holy, knightly order around a missing treasure, perhaps even an unattainable relic such as the Holy Grail, it would be an insensitive king who tried to build his new order around a symbol that each day would remind its members that the land of its origin was far from conquered. And Edward, perhaps more than any monarch before him, was sensitive to the weight and potency of these symbols in the emblematic mind. He would have recognised that, unless he prosecuted a ruinous campaign and somehow managed to conquer Scotland, there would always be a troubling ambiguity about the Scottish cross, a dubiousness about its status. The Welsh cross in comparison was straightforward. Wales was defeated. Wales was the land of Arthur. Therefore it was Y Groes Gneth that Edward chose to gift to the Order of the Garter as its founding relic.

To minister to the Order and its reliquary, Edward instituted a royal chapel in Windsor Castle to house the Croes and to become the Order's ritual home. Known as the Chapel of the Cross Gneth, this foundation would one day evolve into St George's Chapel. And to tend to the relic and steward the souls of the knights, Edward also created a royal college of canons to be overseen by a warden.

The chapel itself was to be sumptuous. Among many rich adornments, Edward commissioned a vast reredos or altar screen to act as the backdrop to Y Groes Gneth. Made from Nottingham alabaster, the reredos was so imposing it had to be brought to Windsor in ten carts drawn by sixty horses. Finally, like Ireland's High King and possibly Scotland's before him, Edward commissioned a new reliquary to hold his fragment of the True Cross.

Y Groes Gneth of Edward's mind's eye would always have been significant enough to dominate the conceptual space of the Order. It was, after all, a fragment of the True Cross in a reliquary of deep antiquity that had been taken in conquest from a noble prince and which demonstrated the divine right of England to rule the lands of Arthur. Yet, from what we can tell, Y Groes Gneth, like the Black Rood, seems originally to have been quite small, made only to encapsulate a splinter of the True Cross. The legend was to grow up that it had been found on the body of the slain Prince Llewelyn, and this suggests that it might have been a personal reliquary, a thing that could be worn, like a locket.

So in 1352, this possibly small object and the embellishments it had already accumulated was taken to London to be made worthy of the magnificence of the

Order of the Garter. A team of international craftsmen led by the king's goldsmith Richard de Grymesby worked on the Cross for nearly two years. They created a new foot or stand of gold and silver, and purchased pearls, rubies and emeralds to embellish it. The entire refit was to cost over £300.

When it returned to Windsor, Y Groes Gneth had been transformed. It was now a monumental Celtic cross, five jewels scintillating upon it, one at the crossing and four at the meeting of the arms with the enclosing circle, like the five wounds of Christ. The only surviving contextual image was painted on a ceiling boss of St George's Chapel over a hundred years later. It shows a golden Croes Gneth backed by a golden sunburst with a kneeling King Edward IV and a kneeling Bishop of Salisbury adoring it on either side. In this incarnation, Y Groes Gneth had become a thing that could hold the eye and the respect of the Kings of England, Scotland and France, the Prince of Wales, the twenty-four knights and the assembly of canons. It was now near the height of a man.

* * *

Almost certainly at the same time, and probably with much of the same fanfare, Edward III seems to have gifted the Black Rood to Durham Cathedral.

The first record of the Black Rood's relocation to Durham occurs in 1383 when Sir Thomas Segbruk, the shrine keeper in the cathedral, created an inventory of all the gifts that had been given to Cuthbert's shrine over the centuries.

> 'In the year of our Lord 1383...' he wrote, 'this book was composed of the relics in the shrine of the saint.... by Sir Thomas Segbruk, then keeper of the shrine, in order to declare what and of what nature the relics... in what place, or upon what step.
>
> In primis: in the first or highest step to the south, an image of the blessed virgin Mary, of silver gilt.
>
> Item, an image... of silver gilt, with a rib of the same, enclosed in the breast of the image.
>
> Item: a black cross called the Black Rode of Scotland...'[10]

Segbruk's decision to compile an inventory would have been related to the installation of a great reredos in Durham. This was commissioned by the son of Lord Neville, the English commander at the Battle of Neville's Cross, to memorialise his father; and although it was now thirty years since the battle, the Durham altar screen may have been a deliberate matching of the reredos commissioned by Edward III to honour Crécy and Y Groes Gneth at the founding of the Order of the Garter. The mirroring suggests that Durham wanted to keep the Black Rood in architectural parity with the Croes, and the altar screen may even have been used to display it.

Segbruk's curation of the relics under his care also reunited, perhaps for the first time in 250 years, the Black Rood with the cross the Durham monks knew as 'the Cross of Saint Margaret'. This was the posthumous gift made perhaps by one of Margaret's sons that was recorded by Reginald, the Durham historian who had written the account of the cathedral's opening ceremony. It was, he had said, a cross 'sparkling in a most wonderful manner with pearls and jewels, which even when dying she held in her hand'.

But if Sir Thomas Segbruk saw any significance in the conjunction of the Black Rood with the Cross of Saint Margaret, he did not remark on it. He may not even have been aware of the connection between the two.

The exact date and circumstance in which the Black Rood arrived in Durham is not recorded however. Four trejectories are possible: that the Black Rood was returned to Scotland as part of the the humiliating treaty of 1328, only to be recaptured from David II at the Battle of Neville's Cross; that a second Black Rood had been created in Scotland after the first had been taken by Edward I and that it was this replacement that was captured at the battle or the Black Rood could have been returned to Scotland by Edward III as a placatory peace offering to David II prior to Edward's invasion of France and then captured at the battle; or the Black Rood could have been gifted by Edward III to Durham Cathedral in celebration and gratitude for the Battle of Neville's Cross.

Whichever trajectory it took, whether it was captured or gifted, the presentation of the Black Rood to Durham Cathedral could not have been something that could have happened without Edward III's approval. And much like his gifts of golden ships after the sea battle of Sluys, what could have been more fitting for as symbolically sensitive and largesse loving a king as Edward III than, at his moment of supreme triumph to give thanks for his twin victories by sacrificing his two totemic crown jewels, each of equal renown, each held in equal regard by his grandfather, each symbolising one of the subjugated nations of Britain, and each sent to a mystical hilltop citadel? One to the north country, the other to the south, in the compass directions of France and Scotland, the lands over which he prosecuted his right to be king. The first, because of its connection to the land of Arthur, went to his new Camelot at Windsor. The other, because of its connection to the land of Scotland, went to Turgot's cathedral shrine in the border stronghold of Durham.

In Durham, the Black Rood could simultaneously act as a reward for the victory of Neville's Cross, and work as a reminder to Bishop Hatfield and to the men of the north country of their obligation to defend the realm against Scotland and stand as a glinting taunt to Scotland of its place in the King's conceptual domain.

11

King Edward VI and Y Groes Gneth

For 200 years after the Battle of Neville's Cross, the Black Rood hung on the wall of Malcolm and Margaret's cathedral like the pelt of a tigress, spread-eagled and splayed like an ornamental tree. The gutted and humiliated trophy of a fierce and noble enemy, it was a provocation to the Scots, and a hostage for the bishops of Durham to hold.

And then, with the Reformation, it disappeared.

The Reformation corroded everything that maintained the existence of the Black Rood, Y Groes Gneth, the Cross of Cong. First, the intellectual underpinnings of belief were dismantled and it became preposterous to many that divine power could be transferred by some mechanism of contact from Christ to the Cross to fragments of that Cross to the reliquaries that contained or had once contained them and so to the supplicants who touched the reliquaries or came into their presence. At the same time, the agency and authority of all the entities of the Church who wielded power was diminished, constrained or denied: from the True Cross to the pope to the hierarchy of archbishops, bishops and priests, to the monks, friars, pardoners and the saints and angels.

And with the intellectual foundations and authority removed, the super-structure of earthly resources was also dismantled: the gold and silver of the crosses, chalices, plates and candlesticks, the jewels, the rich cloths and vestments, the land holdings, the abbeys, their fisheries, tanneries, sheep farms and timber woods, the income form penances, bequests and legacies, all confiscated, ended or sold.

Finally, the actions of people who came to the Church to steward their soul were constrained, with exemplary executions and torture, fines, ostracization and exclusion from public life for all those who would not repudiate their old thinking and behaviour, and embrace the new.

Begun by Henry VIII, continued by his Protestant children, and prosecuted by their successors for more than 200 years, the English Reformation made it impossible for reliquaries of the True Cross to continue to exist. For they were triply vulnerable. Their gold and jewels were to be stripped and taken by the Crown. The relics of the True Cross they contained was to be thrown away like so much mulch or kindling. And their prominence and centrality to the churches that housed them meant they could not be overlooked or forgotten in the chaos of destruction.

Such was the completeness of its removal and the contempt for any record of its existence, we do not know what happened to the Black Rood. However, we can follow what became of Y Groes Gneth.

Y Groes Gneth had retained its profile through the Wars of the Roses and into the reigns of the Welsh Tudors, the Welshness of the reliquary perhaps enhancing its interest to the dynasty. Henry VIII's mother, Elizabeth of York, made offerings to it in the months before she died, and the sister of Catherine of Aragon, Henry VIII's first wife, visited the chapel to venerate it when her husband was invited to join the Order of the Garter. For this visit, Y Groes Gneth was laid out on a 'cushion of cloth of gold'.

Henry VIII even oversaw its further restoration. By 1534, 150 years after it had first been embellished for Edward III by Richard de Grymesby and his team of craftsmen, the Croes needed some restoration. Pilgrims and canons had been picking away at its encrusting jewels and had prised many of them away for their own benefit, in the next world and this. An inventory was made in that year describing its condition.

> *Item: the holy cross clothed in gold garnished with rubies, sapphires, hemerods, lacking of the same stones the number fifteen as that appeareth in the place where they were set. The foot of the cross is all gold costyd [ribbed], standing upon lions garnished full with pearl and stone lacking in the same foot 29 stones and pearls as it appeareth in the place where they stood the which holy cross was at the priory of northern Wales and King Edward III our first founder gave the livelihood to have the holy cross to Windsor, the foot of the cross was 369 ounces and a half.*

Perhaps because it was kept in a royal foundation, Y Groes Gneth avoided being swept up in Henry VIII's initial plundering of the church. However, it did not survive the attentions of his son Edward VI. It is a slight irony of history that it was an Edward who caused Y Groes Gneth to be destroyed. The first Edward captured it; the second saw it used against him; the third embellished and promoted it; the fourth had himself depicted while adoring it; but the sixth Edward – the child king – was the one who ordered its confiscation and destruction.

Edward, his brief administration desperate for liquidity, moved to confiscate all the valuables which were no longer required for use in his Protestant church. 'All such goods were taken away to the King's use; that is to say, all the jewels of gold and silver as crosses, candlesticks, censers, and chalices, and all other gold and silver, and ready money'.

Y Groes Gneth fell into this category and should have been surrendered to the Crown. However, rumours began to circulate that the Dean and other canons of St George's Chapel had not been acting honourably as stewards of the relics and treasures of the Order of the Garter. It was rumoured that they had been selling them off for their own gain.

Edward was personally alert to the concealment of valuables or the profit of their sales. On 12 July 1552, at the age of fifteen, he wrote to the Captain of the Isle of Guernsey to 'take heed to the church plate that it not be stolen away but kept safe till further order be taken'. Then in November he noted in his diary how 'Certain [men] were thought to be sought out by several commissions, viz., whether I was justly answered of the plate, lead, iron, etc. belonged to [the] abbeys; whether I was justly answered [of] the profit of alum, copper, fustians, etc., which were appointed to be sold; and suchlike articles'.

On 16 July 1552, one of his commissions visited Windsor to produce an inventory of all the valuables that remained in the chapel. While its members were there, they happened upon an inventory made only eight years before and so were able to compare the two. The records did not match. Many valuables were missing.

The commission ordered the chapel officials to appear before them to explain the discrepancies between the two documents. However, on the day of the appointment, all the officials were simultaneously taken ill and unable to attend. The commission tried again, with the same result, and eventually demanded a written explanation. This the chapel did provide. In the submission, the officials argued that as the absolute owners of the property they had indeed sold the valuables, but only because they knew of no law that forbade them. They used some of the profit to pay for the installation of a modern plumbing system that would provide running water to their apartments. They then appended a list of everything they had sold off in the previous nine years. The Dean of the College added a helpful personal note, saying that if any more that this had been sold it had been done without his knowledge, as he had been 'in such extreme sickness for the most part of every year' that because of this he had hardly been at Windsor, and had therefore left behind 'his keys and book of statues with the elder Canon then being Resident'.

And here, in a list of items titled 'Parcels of plate put to vendition in the year our Lord 1548' were the dismembered parts of Edward III's Croes Gneth.

Imprimis: the back of the holy cross, being of plate of gold.

Item: a long piece of gold pertaining to the garnishing of the holy cross.

Item: two pieces of loose gold pertaining to the garnishing of the holy cross.

Only the foot or stand created by Richard de Grymesby remained at Windsor 'garnished with sundry stones, many lacking, and also lacking a lion of gold'. These remains were confiscated, taken to the Tower and never heard of again.

Of course, these were only the garnishings, the gold-plate decorations and trimmings that surrounded, complemented and enhanced the relic inside. Yet whether the original reliquary and its fragment of the True Cross were saved we do not know. Nor is there any hint of what happened to them. Y Groes Gneth was obliterated.

The Cross of Cong
© *National Museum of Ireland*

*The reverse of the Cross of Cong,
with its missing gold plate.
© National Museum of Ireland*

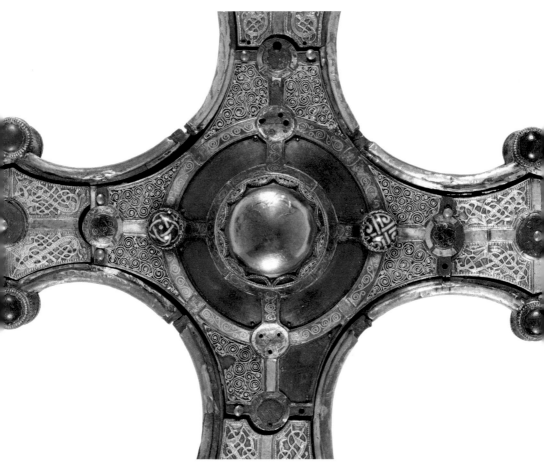

The central boss of the Cross of Cong with its polished rock crystal which once magnified the claimed relic of the True Cross within. Note the missing enamel studs and gold fretwork panels. © National Museum of Ireland

The Fiacail Phadraig (front) – a satchel-shaped shine said to contain a tooth of Saint Patrick, likely made in the same workshop as the Cross of Cong.
© National Museum of Ireland

The Fiacail Phadraig (reverse) © National Museum of Ireland

The shrine of Saint Manchan, also likely made in the same workshop as the Cross of Cong. © National Museum of Ireland

An image of Y Groes Gneth preserved on a boss in the ceiling of St George's Chapel, Windsor. The kneeling figures are King Edward IV and Richard Beauchamp, Bishop of Salisbury and Chancellor of the Order of the Garter. © The Dean and Canons of Windsor

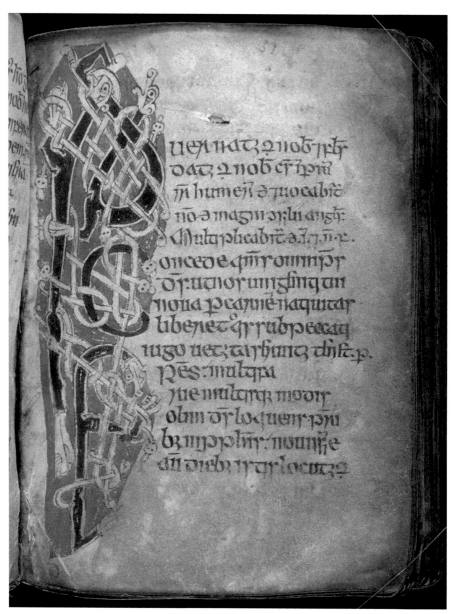

A missal likely to have been created, like the Cross of Cong, for Turlough O'Connor and his new religious centre at Tuam. The decoration is common to both, and they may also have been hidden and rediscovered together. Permission of the President and Fellows of Corpus Christi College Oxford, MS 282, fol.51r

The undocumented Anglo-Saxon equal-armed, gold-and-garnet cloisonné cross, likely a former reliquary, that was found concealed in the coffin of Saint Cuthbert by James Raine in 1827 and which is known as the Cuthbert Cross © Naomi Blayney

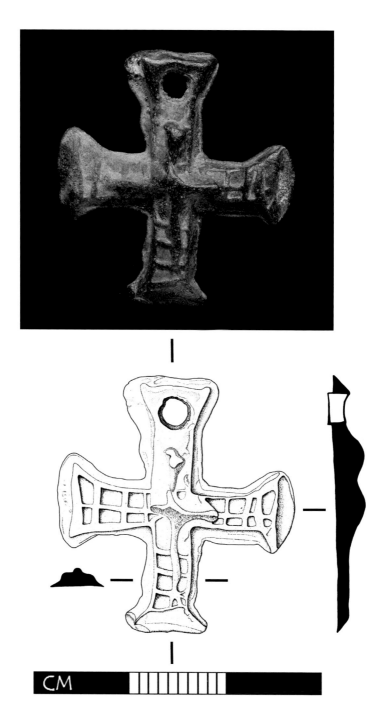

The fourteenth- or fifteenth-century pilgrim badge found in Durham's River Wear in 2012 which is similar to the Cuthbert Cross © Gary Bankhead

12

WILLIAM CLAXTON, KING DAVID II AND THE BLACK ROOD

During the second half of the sixteenth century, a Durham antiquarian named William Claxton took it upon himself to record the architecture, fixtures, decorations and some of the history of Durham Cathedral as they had been before the dissolution of the monastery in 1539. Although not Roman Catholic himself, Claxton's sympathies were with the religion, and he wanted to provide an account of the pre-dissolution cathedral and its precincts before the living memory was lost and what remained of its legacy destroyed. Apart from his own recollection and reconnaissance of the buildings, he studied the books and manuscripts relating to its history that were available to him, consulted with other antiquarians, and recalled the contents of the visitor interpretation boards that had once been set up around the cathedral for pilgrims to read so they could understand the significance of the artefacts they saw around them.

But it was from the former monks and officials that he learned the most. Although Claxton had been only eight or nine years old when the monastery was dissolved, he would have spoken to men such as Edward Pattinson, the cloister porter, Stephen Marley, the former sub-prior or the ex-monk Thomas Spark, all of whom were long enough lived to have helped him with the detail he needed.

Spark had even been present at that defining moment of the Reformation at Durham: the day that Saint Cuthbert's shrine had been destroyed. So it was perhaps from Spark that Claxton learned how King Henry VIII's commissioners had headed straight to the cathedral's sacred *raison d'etre* to smash open Cuthbert's coffin-reliquary.

The last time it is certain that the coffin of Cuthbert had been opened was in the reverential disinterment of 1104, at the opening of the cathedral, when Turgot and the soon-to-be King Alexander I of Scotland had peered down on the lifelike, miraculously preserved body of the saint and seen the gifts that Athelstan, Margaret's great forebear and the first King of all England, had left in his honour.

But while that disinterment had been characterised by respect, hesitancy and then, on discovering the body was still preserved, exultant rejoicing, this examination was brutal. For Spark and the other officials watching, it must have been a visceral horror, like the public execution of a loved one.

Before the Reformation, the coffin of Cuthbert had been housed and venerated on a raised shrine behind the high altar of the cathedral and Claxton reports that having first sent a goldsmith up to strip all the gold and jewels with which the shrine and the coffin were covered, finding, he records, a jewel of such value that it would be 'suffcient to redeem a prince', King Henry's commissioners then directed the goldsmith to break open the iron-bound chest.

Taking up a blacksmith's huge forehammer, the goldsmith swung down and smashed open the lid.

The commissioners and their henchmen were expecting dust and bones, with perhaps a few precious ornaments glinting in the debris that could be snatched up and sent back to Whitehall. Indeed, the goldsmith found beneath the splintered wood some kind of gold staff – a 'metawand' Claxton called it – that had been added to the coffin at some unknown point.

But as he cleared away the mess of wood, searching for more precious metal, the goldsmith uncovered, or so Claxton was to claim, a bearded human face staring back at him.

The goldsmith started back. Looking down the length of the coffin, he realised there was a fully robed body attached to the head and that the first blow of his hammer had broken through the wood and smashed the corpse's leg. Oddly, the goldsmith was chagrined.

'Alas I have broken his leg', he shouted out to his colleagues below.

The commissionaires on the floor of the church at first did not believe him and instructed him to throw down the bones. He then made some attempt to pull the cadaver apart but could not affect it.

One of the commissioners now climbed onto the shrine himself and also tried to pull whatever was left of Cuthbert apart. He shouted something in Latin down to his colleague about the body still being intact.

'If you do not believe me, come up yourself and see him', he added. And now a third investigator clambered up on to the shrine to stare incredulously down at a corpse.

The commissioners were used to dealing with over-revered bones and, after the surrounding valuables and ornaments had been confiscated, they would have usually had them reinterred in mass graves, so preserving both respect for the dead while also preventing specific remains from being re-identified. The fact that Cuthbert's corpse retained enough integrity to make dismemberment difficult gave the commissioners pause.

Claxton recorded the outcome: '...so it happened, contrary their expectation, that not only his body was whole and incorrupt, but the vestments, wherein his body lay, and wherewith all he was accustomed to say mass was fresh, safe and not consumed. Whereupon the visitors commanded that he should be carried to the revestry where he was close and safely kept, in the inner part of the revestry till such time as they did further know the King's pleasure, what to do with him. And upon notice of the King's pleasure therein, the Prior and the monks buried him in the ground under the same place where his shrine had been exalted'.

Claxton does not record what the commissioners did with the Black Rood, he does, however, record what the Black Rood looked like and the stories that were attached to it, offering a last glimpse before it re-entered obscurity.[11]

His descriptions are confused however. Claxton and his informants knew there was some link between the Black Rood and the Battle of Neville's Cross. Oral history had passed down to them traditions about those now 200-year-old events: the monks sent out to parley in fear of their lives; the centrality of the Black Rood to a Scottish king called David's ambition, his founding of Holyrood, and his hiring builders and craftsmen to construct abbeys both there and at Dunfermline; the connection between the capture of King David II and the presentation of the Black Rood to the cathedral. And they tried to bring all these elements together into a single story. There was even a legend that the Black Rood had been taken, like Y Groes Gneth from Llewellyn, from the person of King David, as if it was a wearable thing, like a locket.

So Claxton relayed the story of the two monks who went out to parlay and how they escaped execution by being overlooked in the urgency of the battle. But the oral tradition is subtly different …

> *…a great multitude and number of Scots running and pressing by them both one way and other, with intention to have spoiled them, but yet they had no power or sufferance to commit any violence and force unto such holy persons…*

And Claxton had read how a king of Scots called David had, during an encounter with an ethereal stag, been gifted a relic of the True Cross, and how he had built an abbey called Holyrood in its honour. So he wrote his own version of the story, making the first David the second.

In which said battle, a holy cross which was taken out of the Holy
Roodhouse in Edinburgh in Scotland by King David Bruce was won
and taken upon the said King of Scotland at the said battle, which
cross by most ancient and credible writers is recorded to have come to
the King most miraculously, and to have happened and chanced into
his hand being a hunting at the wild hart in the forest near Edinburgh
upon Holy Rood day, commonly called the exaltation of the cross, the
said King separated and parted from his nobles and company, suddenly
there appeared unto him as it seemed a most fair hart running towards
him in a full and speedy course, which so afraid the king's horse, that he
violently coursed away, whom the hart so fiercely and swiftly followed,
that he bore forcibly both the King and his horse to ground who so being
dismayed did cast back his hand betwixt the tynds of the said hart to
stay himself and then and there more strangely slipped into the King's
hands the said cross most wondrously, at the view whereof immediately
the hart vanished away, and never after was seen. No man knowing
certainly what metal or wood the said cross was made of. In the place
where the miracle was so wrought doth now spring a fountain called
the Rood Well. And the next night after the said cross so bechanced
unto him, the said King was charged and warned in his sleep by a
vision to build an abbey in the same place which he most diligently
observing as a true message from God almighty did send for workmen
into France and Flanders who at their coming were retained and did
build and erect the said abbey accordingly which the King caused to be
furnished with canons regular and dedicated the same in the honour
of the Cross and placed the said Cross most sumptuously and richly in
the said abbey there to remain as a most renowned monument. And
so there remained till the said King coming towards the said battle did
bring it upon him as a most miraculous and fortunate relic.

Claxton also recorded the traditions that remembered the celebrations after
the battle.

And after many conflict and warlike exploits there had been done
between the English and the King of Scots and his company, the said
battle ended and the victory was obtained...

In which battle were slain seven earls of Scotland, besides many earls
and Scottish men, to the number of one and fifteen thousand, but also
lost the said cross. Which was taken upon him, and many together

most worthy and excellent jewels and monuments which were brought from Scotland, as his own banner and other noblemen's ancients [banners]. Which all were offered up at the shrine of St Cuthbert for the beautifying and adoring thereof, together with the Black Rood of Scotland (so termed) …

And Claxton recorded the institutional memory of the arrival of the reliquary in the cathedral and with what ceremony the Black Rood and the other trophies of the battle had been presented.

The King of Scots Ancient and his banner with the Lord Neville's banner, and diverse other noblemen's ancients were all brought to St Cuthbert's feretory (shrine), and there the said Lord Neville after the battle done in most solemn and humble manner did make his petition to God and that holy man St Cuthbert within the feretory to accept his offerings and did offer the aforesaid jewels and banners and the holy rood cross which was taken on the King of Scots to the shrine of that holy and blessed man St Cuthbert within the Feretory; and so after his orisons performed to God and St Cuthbert he departed and there the said banners and ancients did stand, and hung until the suppression of the house…

Finally, in its last record, Claxton described the Black Rood. And although some of his other subject matter is written in the present tense, describing monuments and artefacts that had escaped destruction or confiscation, his description of the Black Rood is tellingly in the past.

At the east end of the south alley, adjoining to the pillar next St Cuthbert's feretory, next to the choir door on the south side, there was a most fair rood or picture of our Saviour, called the Black Rood of Scotland with the picture of Mary and John being brought out of Holyrood house in Scotland by King David Bruce, and was won at the battle of Durham with the picture of our lady on one side of our Saviour and the picture of St John on the other side, the which Rood and pictures were all three very richly wrought in silver, the which were all smoked black over, being large pictures of a yard and five quarters long, and on every one of their heads, a crown of pure beaten gold of goldsmith's work with a device or rest to take them off or on. And on the backside of the said rood and pictures, there was a piece of work that they were fastened unto being all adorned with fine wainscot work and curious paintings well befitting such costly pictures from the middle pillar up to the height of the vault, the which wainscot was all red varnished over very finely, and all set full of stars of lead, every star finely gilded over with gold, and also the said rood and pictures had every of them an iron stuck fast in the back part of the said images that had a hole in the said irons, that went through the wainscot to put in a pin of iron to make them fast to the wainscot.

* * *

It is difficult, however, to reconcile Claxton's description of the Black Rood with any that have gone before. While the Black Rood described by David I's steward Aelred, the one that opened 'like a box' was also a crucifix, there was no doubt that that reliquary was made of gold and not silver, and that at the length of a palm it could not be confused with Claxton's Rood over a yard in height.

In 1307, at the death of Edward I, the reliquary known as the Black Rood was described as being 'of gold-work with a gold chain, in a wooden case with a silver gilt exterior'; the presence of the chain suggested this was something that could be hung near an altar, or around a neck, like a locket.

It is even challenging to reconcile Claxton's description of the Black Rood with his references to it in his own work. He does not attempt to reconcile the cumbersome size of his wall-mounted Rood with the kind of wearable, personal reliquary that might reasonably be 'taken upon' the body of a king or that might have 'chanced into his hand' from between the antlers of an ethereal stag.

Perhaps this Black Rood was a replacement, a monumental Rood created by the Bruce dynasty to hold the piece of the True Cross that had been kept back from Edward I.

Perhaps the Durham monks, seeing the manner in which Y Groes Gneth at Windsor has been embellished and expanded by Edward III, decided to re-appoint and re-present their own royal reliquary, commissioning a sliver rood-case or expanding on its existing silver container to give the Black Rood and the relic some of the same weight and dignity as its Welsh cousin. Perhaps with this further layer of encasement they wanted to remind the world of the honour that the gift from the King had done to their monastery, of their role in that year of English triumph and of their parity in the King's esteem.

Perhaps it was just a simple mistake by Claxton or his informant, one that, like his mixing up of the two Davids, went uncorrected because Claxton died before his life's work was complete. An authorial draft of the manuscript still exists, written in his own Elizabethan secretary hand, the sheets of paper showing evidence of being sewn together as Claxton attempted to re-order his complex, evolving materials into a coherent whole. Perhaps he died mid-edit having got it wrong.

13

FATHER PRENDERGAST AND THE CROSS OF CONG

In Ireland too, the Cross of Cong vanished, its fall from grace being even more precipitous. Only a very few years after it had been made, the conditions for a True Cross reliquary that spoke to a divine recognition of an insular Irish kingdom became impossible, and the presence of the Cross and its weight in the world was ratcheted down into nothingness.

The title of the High Kingship that O'Connor had dedicated his life to obtaining became meaningless only fifty years after his death, when the King of England took for himself the title of Lord of Ireland and tried to rule the country remotely through a government in Dublin and an importation of Norman adventurers. In time, that English royal lordship hardened into a kingship, and the King of Ireland became a style of title held by the person of the King of England in personal union with his other crowns. That union in its turn led to the attempted imposition of the Protestant church with the importation of Protestant peoples and policies, and ultimately a series of penal laws imposed on the Catholic population which excluded them, unless they recanted, from inheritance, government, professions, public office, university, intermarriage, the franchise, religious leaderships. And, with more turns of the screw, that personal union eventually became a legal amalgamation, with an Act of Union joining the Kingdom of Ireland to that of Scotland and England.

And at each of these junctures – from the jealousy of other kings to the satisfaction of their avarice, through to their insistence on conformity to their beliefs – whoever was the guardian of the Cross of Cong recognised both its value and its vulnerability saw that it might be stolen, hostaged or destroyed, and so diminished its importance and quietened its existence so as not to provoke its removal, until, like the Black Rood and Y Groes Gneth, its presence in the world was entirely obliterated.

81

* * *

By the early nineteenth century, the parish priest at Cong, a small town in Connacht, still held the grandiose title of Abbot of the Royal Abbey of Cong, although the once-important abbey had been suppressed centuries before and was now a pile of stones. The so-called abbot's name was Father Prendergast and he lived in a cottage about two miles from the edge of town. His occasional visitors would marvel at the authenticity and picturesque charm of his reduced circumstances: 'A small but neat thatched cottage, almost buried in a little wooded dell', one tourist wrote, 'a perfect wilderness of rocks and trees, through which we must wind along a little rugged path, barely wide enough to permit a horse to force his way, and presenting in several elevated points most romantic vistas of Lough Corrib, with its many islands, and the long line of distant mountains that constitute its background'.

Father Prendergast was always courteous to these occasional visitors winding their way along the path from Cong. He would greet them warmly, read their letters of introduction with interest and return their cordiality. One of his regular, uninvited guests was the young son of one of the local Protestant gentry, a William Wilde, who would visit Father Prendergast and listen to his stories of the past glories of Cong Abbey. Later in life, William would remember him as 'a very fine, courteous white-haired old man' and perhaps the boy took a youthful patrician and proprietorial interest in the old priest, for there was a family legend that William's ancestors had, after the abbey had been suppressed and its wealth sold, granted the last monks who had been driven out of the monastery the little area of farmland with its tiny cottages in which Father Prendergast now lived, and which became known as Abbotstown.

The young William would sit with the old priest in his little sitting room and Father Prendergast would open his three-cornered cupboard and, with great pride, draw out the ancient treasures that he had taken into his care.

One of these treasures was a piece of discoloured linen. Father Prendergast would tell William how this unprepossessing rag had been dipped in the very blood of Charles I at his execution in Whitehall and that it retained the Stuart kings' ability to cure scrofula, or the king's evil, and indeed William could testify that hundreds of local people had over the years asked Prendergast to touch them and so transfer the healing power to them.

Another treasure that Father Prendergast kept in his cupboard was the Fiacail Phadraig, the satchel-shaped reliquary that contained the supposed tooth of Saint Patrick. It too was used to perform cures, and, when he was older, William wrote down the story Father Prendergast had told him about how he had acquired it:

how he had 'taken it from a man named Reilly, about fifty years before, a native of Sligo, who made a living by going about this part of the country performing cures upon man and beast'.

'Ladies and ewes are said to have held it in especial repute', wrote William, 'and far and near the population and the flocks were the better of the blessed tooth. One day the old abbot met the custodian of the shrine, and asked him to show him the Fiacail. "Whose is this?" said the priest, when he had it in his possession. "It belonged", said Reilly, "to the canons of Cong". "Then", said Father Prendergast, "I am the last of the Augustinian canons of that monastery, and I'll keep it"; and so, to the amazement of the owner, he rode off with it'.

Finally, Father Prendergast would tell William how, long ago, Saint Patrick had brought to Ireland a piece of the True Cross, and how the saint had left it in the safe keeping of the Augustinian order at Cong and how the piece of the True Cross had been preserved in a cross-shaped reliquary and hidden along with a mass of ancient manuscripts and deeds. And then he would tell William how he himself had rediscovered it, hidden in an oak chest in a cottage in town. And then he would impress the young William by laying in front of him this reliquary of the True Cross, fashioned by Mael Isu and dedicated to the High King of Ireland.

Although its gold still glittered and its central rock crystal still allowed him to glimpse the murky piece of the True Cross within, William could see from its dilapidated state that Father Prendergast's treasure had to be very old. Flecks of the gilt surface had broken off over the years and there were empty sockets and panels where there must once have been glass or enamel studs or plates of gold-filigree. And, although some animal-head pins were still in place, many were missing and some of those that remained had lost their coloured glass eyes. And it was not only the smaller elements, even some of the larger cast-bronze plates on the back were loose or missing, like a shabby jacket with the panels ripped away to reveal the lining.

The manuscripts that had been hidden with it had also gone missing. Father Prendergast told William how, while he was out one time, a tailor, who was working in the cottage, had 'laid hands on the vellum books, and cut them into strips for measures'.

Another of Father Prendergast's visitors was given a different story about the manuscripts. 'A great portion of the valuables thus hidden consisted of deeds of grants of lands to the abbey, and of Irish manuscripts in vellum splendidly illuminated', the visitor recalled. 'It grieves me to add, that these no longer exist. The Abbot, as he confesses, being at the time ignorant of the value of such remains, thought little about them, and on going to the Continent shortly after to improve his education, carelessly left them in the charge of a young priest whom he appointed to do his duty during his absence. He remained abroad eleven years, during which time he found the most ancient and valuable manuscripts which he saw on the Continent appear to resemble, but not equal in beauty, those he has left at home. Thus awakened to a sense of their value, we may imagine, what at least ought to have been, his astonishment and horror, on finding on his return home. that his deputy had during his absence lost or destroyed all those curious and valuable remains – the Cross excepted; and that, unfortunately, the very beauty of the manuscripts had been a chief cause of their destruction, the ignorant young man having cut them up to decorate his breviaries et cetera, with the illuminated letters which they contained'.

And when Father Prendergast died, his cross experienced its own final indignity. '... it was removed to Cong', William, who was about fourteen at the time, records. 'At which time the central crystal had been removed and was usually carried by a lady in her pocket. If still in existence, it is not known where the relique for which the cross was made is at present. It must have been a very small fragment....'

* * *

But for a single exception, there had been no record of the Cross of Cong for 700 years. We do not know how its guardians kept the Cross so quiet for so long. Between its creation in Mael Isu's royal workshop at Roscommon in the twelfth century and its re-emergence in Father Prendergast's three-cornered cupboard in the hamlet of Abbotstown in the nineteenth century, only a single record speaks of its existence. The first Celtic dictionary, the Archeologia Britannica, published in 1707, records a transcription of a part of Mael Isu's dedication along the side of what the Dictionary calls 'the Abbot of Cong's Cross'. The dedication was transcribed in 1680, so it is possible that the Cross survived until then as a publicly-visible or at least privately-held but not fully-hidden artefact and that it was therefore secreted for only a hundred years, from the late seventeenth century to the end of the eighteenth, and that the knowledge of where it was located had been passed down abbot-to-abbot, guardian-to-guardian, and that Prendergast knew where to look. On the other hand, the lack of any repair to the Cross also suggests that no one with the means and status to commission a refurbishment had been in possession of it for a very long time.

When William first encountered the Cross of Cong, all Mael Isu's craftsmanship was coming undone. The Cross of Cong was falling apart, deconstructing itself as the wood of its structural core aged and dried, losing its grip on the nails and pins that held its plates and baubles to itself, shedding its bright gems and gold until all that was left would be that slither of unremarkable, but bloodied wood that had once borne the weight of all human meaning and which would soon disappear into dust.

And perhaps there is some sense that this deconstruction of the Cross and even the manuscripts was not quite the dereliction it seemed but a final act of guardianship by Father Prendergast or the community who believed in the miracle working power of the relic and the things that had been hidden with it, and who had protected it for generations. That by allowing the Cross to finally come apart and sharing out its elements among the faithful, they were in some way preserving the power it once held. It is obvious too, from Father Prendergast's tales of the healing properties of the Fiacail Phadraig and the King's Evil, and from the evidence of other Irish relics, that, far from Henry VIII's Whitehall Palace and the promulgations of his successors, the beliefs of medieval kings and queens had been retained and had continued to evolve among the people whom Prendergast served. They believed, like Margaret, that relics could heal; like Edward, that relics could bear witness to and solemnise oaths; that the Cross could act in the world. So in this way, the distribution of the elements of the Cross – the central crystal, the bronze open-work plates, the crossing plate on the reverse, the numerous glass and enamel jewels, the animal-head pins – might in Prendergast's guardian-successor's mind have been some kind of community preservation.

When William grew into adulthood, he retained his enthusiasm for the antiquarian. While building a career as an eminent surgeon, he recorded the folklore, the cures and charms of his patients, which the scientific method of his medicine was beginning to replace, sometimes taking his son Oscar with him on archaeological investigations. And men like William Wilde, men of the Protestant ascendancy with the leisure and resources to pursue their interests and prosecute their new beliefs, went about the country buying up the metalwork and manuscripts that were re-emerging with the relaxing of the anti-Catholic laws, and placing these curios in their public and private collections. It is likely that one of Father Prendergast's manuscripts somehow survived becoming a tailor's measure and ended up in the Bodleian Library (see the illustration of the Corpus Missal).

In time, they came for the Cross of Cong itself. Father Prendergast's successor, Michael Waldron, seemed content to let the Cross of Cong go, but his parishioners refused. In September 1838 he wrote to the prospective purchaser to explain.

Cong 3 September 1838

My Dear Sir

Your letter of 27th August – from Westport reached me only on the morning of the day you were to leave for Dublin, I therefore thought it more advisable to write to you to Baggot Street.

The people without a single exception would sooner sell all they have in this world then consent to part with the old cross, they actually got furious at the very thought of it, with all their poverty they offered to make up the sum offered for it without delay, tho the only commodity the greater part of them have at present for market is the potatoe and mind not enough of that root for the years supply, they also before they separated got into a subscription to create a fund to have it sent to Dublin to have it repaired and cleaned and to have any of the pebbles that have been lost replaced by new ones, so enthusiastick are their feelings towards any relick of the Abbey as considering it an existing monument of their splendour in olden times that they will insist on getting back Patrick's Tooth cost what it may. –

I regretted much to have heard that the priest of Clifden was in Galway when you went through his district –

If at any at any future period you or any friend of yours or of Mr Kelly's should happen to pass Cong I shall feel great pleasure in having a bed for any such, but please recollect and tell Mr Kelly that the better way would be to write to me by post a few days before their arrival as without this precaution I may not be at home when they arrive as in a county parish of 9 miles in length I am more from home than otherwise both as in the official and in the hospitable way –

I have the honour to be

My Dear Sir

Very truly Yrs.

M. Waldron

P.S. Our Bishop passes by hear next week. I will consult him about the Cross, I wd prefer the price of it for some decorations for the Chapel to itself. We may still prevail on them –

The Cross however was not being purchased for any private collection of antiquities. The buyer was working on behalf of the Royal Irish Academy and the Cross was to be the centrepiece of its new museum of antiquities so forming, alongside the Tara torcs, the nucleus of what was intended to be a national collection, one that what would one day become the National Museum of Ireland.

The large gold fretwork plates that were missing from the back of the Cross were sought out and all but one was located and re-adhered to it (see the illustration of the back of the Cross of Cong), and the Cross began to emerge once more into the light and take on a new meaning. The craftsmanship and unequivocal date of construction of the Cross of Cong demonstrated to the world the sophistication and capabilities of pre-Norman Ireland, and it became an emblem of nationalist pride that such an artefact could be produced entirely independently in an insular Irish kingdom. Its appearance in the Dublin exhibition of 1853 brought the Cross together with other church metalwork and allowed the interested to appreciate the connection between the Cross of Cong and the Shrine of Saint Manchan, and speculate on the workshops of the High King. The exhibition also stimulated the interest of craftspeople, artists and designers who recreated and redeveloped the designs and decorations they saw there, precipitating the so-called Celtic revival and re-using the ancient motifs to create some of the design-signatures of contemporary Irishness. Replicas of the Cross of Cong were made and went around the world – to the Chicago World's Fair of 1853, to churches in Australia and England, to the Metropolitan Museum of Art in New York – and one of these replicas was used by Pope John Paul II for the Papal Mass in Phoenix Park in 1979. Today, the Cross of Cong remains one of the selection of key artefacts in the visitor section known as the Treasury within the National Museum of Ireland.

Like some strange enactment of the fate of the True Cross in the poem the Dream of the Rood, the Cross of Cong had been resurrected, raised up and reclad with gold to shine again.

> *One buried us in deep pit, yet of me the thanes of the Lord,*
>
> *His friends, heard tell; [from earth they raised me],*
>
> *And me begirt with gold and silver.*
>
> *Now thou mayst hear, my dearest man,*
>
> *That bale of woes have I endured,*
>
> *Of sorrows sore. Now the time is come,*

That me shall honor both far and wide
Men upon earth, and all this mighty creation
Will pray to this beacon. On me God's Son
Suffered awhile; so glorious now
I tower to Heaven, and I may heal
Each one of those who reverence me

Epilogue: Durham in 1827 and 2012

On the morning of the 17 May 1827, in the cathedral church of Durham, the Reverend William Gilly was celebrating the morning service in the choir of the Norman building, when he heard a banging and scraping from behind the high altar. Straining to make sense of the noise through the congregation's hymns and prayers, Gilly became increasingly perturbed.

No one in Chapter had mentioned that any building work was being undertaken in the cathedral; and, in any case, there was nothing in that part of the church that he could think of that might require attention. For behind the high altar was the area that had once, long ago, been the shrine of the seventh-century Saint Cuthbert and which now, supposedly, was the site of his grave.

The banging and scraping continued through the service, and, as Gilly strained to listen, he began to discern the muffled exclamations of men. Suppressing his curiosity until the end of the service, as soon as it was over, and without even troubling to change out of his vestments, Gilly ran out of the choir and into the space behind the high altar.

Here, Gilly was astonished to see a dark hole had been created in the pavement of the former shrine. The heavy nine-by-four-foot slab of marble capping the site of the supposed grave had been dragged away, and what lay in its place was a black aperture into the foundations of the cathedral. Two men were standing over the hole while another two workmen were already down in the void itself, trampling on its contents and passing up to their comrades above a mess of what Gilly would later realise were fragments of coffins and human bones.

The two above-ground Gilly knew well. They were William Darnell, who was supposed to be in temporary charge of the cathedral while it was without a presiding dean, and James Raine, the cathedral's librarian, who appeared to be directing the operation.

89

Gilly's arrival, in haste and in his surplice, threw the four men into chagrined confusion, and Gilly took charge. Ordering the two workmen out of the stone-lined grave, he remonstrated with his colleagues, asking what they thought they were doing. Had someone from the town even been consulted? Or, for that matter, should someone from the nearby Roman Catholic college not be informed? Because, after all, whatever remains might still be down there, they were surely relics of their faith and so theirs to honour? The answer to both questions was no. But Gilly detected in Darnell a nervousness and a lack of ease next to Raine's evident determination. No, Darnell said, he wanted no one else to hear about what was happening. He was concerned that if the news got out that Saint Cuthbert's grave had been opened, a crowd might gather that they would not be able to control.

Working out how to proceed, the five men looked down into the crypt-like void and began to make out what the librarian Raine would later call a 'dark substance' occupying the bottom of the grave.

The only natural light they had to aid them came through the clear glass of the rose window that broke through the east wall of the cathedral. With the waxing and waning of the spring sunshine, and with the swirling of the raised dust of hundreds of years, it took a moment for them to discern that the dark thing below them had the eerie shape of a man. A moment longer and they realised that what they were looking down upon was a skeleton, its feet pointing to the east, robed in the vestments of a medieval priest. The brow of the skeleton's skull was visible, and the ends of its shins and the disjointed collapsed bones of its feet were poking out from beneath its shrouds. The skeleton's right arm was folded across its chest where the bones of its hands lay collapsed and confused. It was as if it was attempting to raise its fingers in benediction, as if it wanted to greet them and bless the light of the world into which it was re-emerging.

In the end, it was Gilly, not Raine, who was the first to go down into the grave to examine the skeleton.

Leaving behind the fresh spring air of Georgian Durham, he lowered himself into the hole. And now he was nearer to the remains, Gilly could see something new. He peered closer. Among the wreck of dusky wood, the pale, protruding bones, the mouldering vestments, he began to discern the remnants of colour. There were faded ambers, crimsons, purples and greens in the vestments, patterns that resolved themselves into birds, beasts, fish and flowers. And something was shimmering here and there among the robes and bones. There were golden and silver sparkles in the gloom. Leaning down, he saw a gold sheen on the brow of the skull, and gold wire wrapped around it like a crown of thorns. More threads of gold wire had been embroidered into some of the vestments, and a panel of silver-covered wood was laid out on the skeleton's chest. And nestling alongside the silver, glimmering in the half light, there was something that should not have been there. Something wonderful.

Gilly reached down and drew from the folds of the robes a small cross made of gold and red garnets (see the illustration of the Cuthbert Cross). One of its tiny arms was broken, but, scooping up the pieces, he saw that he held in his hands an intricately crafted, gold and jewelled cruciform pendant.

The remnants of a silken cord twisted with gold wire were left scintillating in its place, as if the cross had once been hung around the neck of the skeleton, like a locket.

* * *

When he was at his leisure, James Raine, the cathedral librarian, had the opportunity to study the cross Gilly had picked out from what he was now certain were the bones of Saint Cuthbert. The cross was tiny, only two and three-eighths of an inch across at its widest point. A small equal-armed cross made of gold and red garnets, its arms were thin and curved, and the whole thing had a raised, architectural quality, so much so that when viewed from the side, the cross took on the shape and proportions of a fortress, with the central garnet serving as a domed rotunda.

Raine weighed the cross, noting it was fifteen pennyweights and twelve grains, and he remarked on its ungold-like appearance, commenting, 'The cross is of gold – but the gold appears to have undergone some process, tending to deaden its lustre, for its dingy appearance can scarcely be the effect of time'.

But the first, most obvious thing about the cross was that it had been broken. Raine or his daughter made a line drawing of the condition in which it was found. 'The arm which stands the lowest upon my engraving was found broken off', he wrote, 'and upon examination, it appeared to have been broken once before, as there were evident proofs that it had been repaired by means of small rivets, some of which were remaining'. The attacks had obviously been violent, for these rivet holes had been torn open, ripping the gold baseplate, tearing open one of the four garnet settings around the central jewel, dislocating the garnet it housed, and forcing another five garnets out of their frames on the detached arm. It was as if someone had thought there was something inside the cross and had needed to recover it urgently. Or it had been fought over.

There was also evidence of violence at the base of the loop at the top through which the neck chain, or what Raine described as a 'silken cord twisted with gold', would have passed. The metal at the bottom of this loop had been torn, as if the cross had been yanked from where it was hanging, either around the neck of its owner or from above an altar. This action had damaged the suspension loop to such an extent that it had been replaced.

So the cross was small and deep, and had a violent history. Looking more closely under a magnifying glass and when viewed from the side, Raine would have seen that it was designed like some crusader castle, with lines of crenelations and fortifications rising in stepped courses from the base to culminate in a great central dome, as if it were a fortress protecting something.

Built on a base plate made of gold, the lowest ground-level feature was a beaded gold wire that skirted the first rising wall of gold running around the entire perimeter of the cross. Above this course was a curved moulding topped by another beaded wire. The line of this feature was interrupted twice along the side arms, and again at the corners and centres of the arm-ends, by what looked for all the world like domed turrets punctuating the curtain walls of a fortress, but which on examination were found to be the sheaths and heads of false rivets. At the join of the arms with the central rotunda were four larger drum towers with high gold walls which were roofed over with single red garnets – it was one of these which had been ripped out when the structure had been breached. Another golden wall sitting above the first brought the structure of the arms above the level of the watch towers and this was then itself topped by a line of dogtooth crenelations. The sharp ends of the teeth pointed outwards and, like the beaded wires, this embellishment created bright points of reflected light and deep chasms of shadow that baffled the eye, producing a shimmering, indistinct effect and disguising the solidity of the architectural form. Above this course was another beaded wire which gave on to the narrow flat roofs of the four arms. The roofs themselves were each formed from a cloisonné pavement of twelve dark-red garnets with thin veins of gold running between them – the number corresponding to that of Christ's disciples, the red to His blood. The curve of the arms was so great that the cloisonné cells could only be laid two layers deep at each of the arm ends but which then narrowed to a single layer between the two concave curves. So close to overlapping were the curves that the sides of the two arms almost touched in the middle.

Looming above the arms and rising to twice their height was the central rotunda. This was built up above the plane of the arms by concentric rising steps of curtain wall, beaded wire and dog-tooth battlements. This circular mount culminated in a plateau of white shell, on top of which, and taking up almost all the available surface, stood the final fitting. Set in three layers of beaded moulding and a final curving slope of gold, the great dome of the rotunda was made of a single large red garnet.

The finding of the cross was intriguing. Like Turgot's friend Symeon before him, James Raine knew his history, and, as the cathedral librarian, he had access to all the original records concerning Cuthbert and his shrine. But, as he worked his back through the parchments, manuscripts and other records in preparation for the writing of his book about the exhumation, Raine could find nothing that accounted for the cross being there. Everything else that he, Gilly, Darnell and the other men had found that day had some kind of provenance in the history of Cuthbert and his relics. The coffins had been well described in the histories; the rich, silk vestments were known to have been reverentially placed on the corpse by Turgot in 1104 in the presence of the future Alexander III; the embroideries and braidings with the gold threads that Gilly had seen glittering in the grave were surely those that had been recorded as gifts from King Athelstan in the tenth century; the comb had been noted before; the small personal altar made of wood with its laminar of silver that Gilly found had been seen by Alexander. Only the cross was unexpected and surprising. Raine knew enough about Anglo-Saxon metalwork to be certain that the cross was as old as Cuthbert himself but where could it have come from? That such a magnificent cross could have been gifted to the shrine and placed on the corpse without the event being recorded was impossible for Raine to imagine, so he felt obliged to provide an explanation. It was, he opined, Cuthbert's personal cross, perhaps, later commentators would claim, even the cross he wore as Bishop of Lindisfarne. What else could it be?

It is not known whether Raine noted another aspect of the cross that was not quite as it should be. He did not remark on it. But there was something about that central setting that was not quite right. The central garnet all but obscured the layer of pearly shell to which it was fixed. And this shell pavement, despite its expense, could only just be seen as a thin ring of chalky white circling the somewhat lumpen central stone. Like a ring of white puss surrounding a blood blister, the shell gave the cross the appearance of a bull's eye, a visual trope that did not complement the intricate sophistication of the underlying design. What was more, beneath its gold collar, where it could not be seen, the shell layer had been hacked about to fit the hole it covered. A later examiner of the cross was even to suggest this central boss, with its crudely cut shell and misshapen central garnet, could even have been taken from another piece of Anglo-Saxon jewellery and been added to the cross when the original central fitting had to be replaced for some reason.

All of this, Raine was to discover, was like the Cross of Cong in that it had been built around a cavity. Hidden beneath the central garnet and its shell floor was a gold-lined void formed within a vertical, circular sleeve of sheet gold, a quarter of an inch high. The space was empty.

It was as if the cross had been designed as a reliquary, to cherish the most precious and holy of somethings beneath its central garnet, something that was no longer there.

* * *

As the years, decades and centuries passed, other equal-armed gold and garnet cloisonné crosses from the same early Christian period were discovered in England: at Wilton in the 1850s; at Ixworth in 1856; at Holderness in 1965; and at Trumpington in 2011. And archaeologists began to realise that, where they could be determined, these crosses, just like the disc brooches from which they derived, were only ever found in the graves of women. And as their ability to date the graves themselves became more and more precise, archaeologists also noticed that the deposition of grave goods like the Cuthbert Cross had all but ended by the date of his death. And while James Raine's hypothesis that it must be Cuthbert's personal cross remained just about reasonable, Cuthbert was becoming too old and too male to have been buried with such a cross.

Then on Monday 9 May 2011, a curious trinket in the style of an equal-armed cloisonné cross was pulled out of the river at Durham (see the illustration of the Bankhead pilgrim badge). It was found by underwater archaeologist, Gary Bankhead, who was working his way down through the striated gullies that had been ice-scoured into the bedrock of the river. These gullies, some of which could be up to a meter in depth, had been collecting silt and debris washed along by the river for millennia. Most recently, during Durham's industrial heyday, iron in the water had interacted with riverbed sediment to create a solid concretation over the gullies, sealing them off like a scab. The area Gary was excavating lay just downstream of the medieval Elvet Bridge, and the gullies there were rich in archaeological finds as they had been filled with numerous small objects that had been thrown or dropped from the bridge and the busy riverbanks of the city.

The trinket cross was found alongside other items from the fourteenth and fifteenth centuries. Two of these finds were hammered silver coins, one from the reign of Edward III and the other from that of Edward IV, suggesting the cross was late medieval in origin. It looked and felt like a pilgrim badge – an inexpensive souvenir of a visit to a shrine that would be pinned to the hats of pilgrims or hung from their necks in pride and proof of their visit, or perhaps bought in pairs, one of which to be cast into a river as a votive offering in hopes of a safe return home.

A cross is a cross is a cross. But it was the shape and contours of his find that excited Gary. 'I knew what it was as soon as I brought it to the surface', he said. 'It looked like the Cuthbert cross'.

Made of medieval quality pewter, the cross was, according to Gary's find report, a 'cast lead alloy object in the form of a pectoral cross, with equal length flaring arms; the front face features decoration representative of the Anglo-Saxon cloisonné cell work. The rear face is undecorated with a flat plain surface. The

94

object's style has parallels with four seventh-century cross pendants from the early Christian period found in England, all displaying cloisonné inlays for garnets. However, the closest parallel is with the seventh century St Cuthbert pectoral cross with its simple square cut garnet inlays'.

The workmanship is crude, and perhaps it is even a reject. Where the Cuthbert Cross found by William Gilly and James Raine has an apostolic twelve cloisonné cells on each arm, the arms of the pilgrim badge has just eight or ten. Where the silhouette of the Cuthbert Cross is defined by the tight sweeping curves formed by the interlocking circles of its underlying design, the pilgrim badge has wide irregular castling flanges around its arms, as if too much molten alloy had accidentally been poured into the mould and then not cut away or filed down after it had cooled. Where the Cuthbert Cross has a raised boss made of a single large garnet, the pilgrim badge has an amorphous globular shape ranging over its central area, suggesting to Gary that the bottom of the clay mould into which the molten pewter was poured had failed during manufacture, with the liquid metal seeping into the crumbling clay and destroying the detail of the cross's centre.

'It is reasonable to assume therefore', wrote Gary, 'that because of the object's design flaws it was deemed unsellable and was thrown by the vendor or pedlar into the river below: rather than being re-used'.

Someone in Durham, in the fourteenth or fifteenth century, was manufacturing pewter badges to sell to pilgrims that were made to the design of an equal-armed cloisonné-celled cross, and one of them ended up in the river beneath the cathedral in Durham, where one day a real equal-armed cloisonné cross would be found.

AFTERWORD

What happened to the Black Rood?

The simplest explanation is that it was taken away like Llewelyn's Croes Gneth, its jewels flicked out, its gold melted down, its claimed portion of the True Cross thrown away.

But is there any possibility that it could be like Turlough O'Connor's Cross of Cong: secreted away, its hiding place known only to a few former monks, handed down, the secret lost or at least unverified, waiting to be fetched out of hiding by some mild-mannered Father Prendergast or aggressively enterprising James Raine?

The possibility is real not only because of the example of the Cross of Cong. The secretion of valuables during the Reformation seems to have been as common in Durham as Edward VI would have suspected. As early as 1532, his father's first wave of commissioners found a 'very secret place' in Durham Abbey where £300 had been hidden. Hugh Whitehead, the last man to hold Turgot's position of Prior, and the first professed Protestant Dean of the cathedral, was himself accused of holding back £70 worth of monastic vessels. Like Spark, Whitehead had been one of the handful of cathedral officials who had watched on as Cuthbert's coffin had been ransacked by Henry VIII's commissioners, and several years later in 1551, just after the investigation into the selling of Y Groes Gneth, he was to be accused of hiding a 'great quantity of treasure' in his chamber. A warrant was issued and Whitehead was imprisoned but died before he could appear in front of the court.

Far from Whitehall, far from Windsor, far from the king's gaze, valuables and artefacts that should have been destroyed or surrendered would reappear.

The so-called Ring of Saint Cuthbert, made of solid gold and a sapphire, which was seen on the saint's hand while his remains lay out in the Revestry waiting on the King's pleasure, escaped the attention of the commissioners and survived, handed down, monk to monk in secret reverence until it was safe to be revealed. Two altar stones, which would have contained relics, were dug out of their hiding places during the 1569 Rising of the North, along with two holy-water stoops which were temporarily restored to the cathedral entrance. And the Banner of Saint Cuthbert – an artefact said to have been constructed to hold a cloth found in the coffin of the saint in 1104 – also reappeared, only to be burned, according to Claxton, by the wife of a later Protestant dean.

In this context, the misidentification of the Black Rood in Claxton's remembrance of the pre-Reformation cathedral may even be a clue. It is such an odd mistake given the weight the Black Rood has in his stories about the Battle of Neville's Cross. So perhaps Claxton was being deliberately misleading or had himself been misled, and the true Black Rood with its portion of the True Cross had been hidden from the commissioners, with the larger Rood serving as a decoy in case they ever asked what had happened to it.

And what are we then to make of the undocumented Anglo-Saxon gold-and-garnet cloisonné cross which was found in Cuthbert's grave in 1827 and which has become known as the Cuthbert Cross? It cannot be David I's reliquary described by Aelred: a gold crucifix with an ivory carving of Christ which was the length of a palm and which opened like a box. But the descriptions of Edward I's trophy Black Rood – 'of gold-work with a gold chain' – is vague enough to fit, as it would more or less any suspendable gold cross.

And what then of the pilgrim badge? If it was, as Gary Bankhead suggests, a reject that was tipped into the river in Durham, that meant it was being manufactured there. This not only enhances the possibility that it is a representation of the Cuthbert Cross – for how many equal-armed cloisonné crosses might Durham possess? But it also creates a conundrum. Because it suggests there was a market, a medieval demand for memorabilia of a visit to the cathedral, and this means the cross being depicted must have been famous enough to satisfy that demand, and so it must have been visible enough in Durham to make visitors want to take one home a souvenir. So what cross could it have been?

For me, at the time of writing, Gary Bankhead's pilgrim badge tips the balance of probabilities. For the Cuthbert Cross to have had anything to do with the living Cuthbert, so many people would have had to have failed to see it: Spark, Whitehead, the commissioners, their goldsmith with his great forehammer, Turgot, Alexander, the ear-shaking Abbot of Séez, the twelfth-century monks who informed Reginald and another writer about the opening of the cathedral, King Athelstan while leaving his own gifts, the eighth-century monks who informed Bede and Cuthbert's first anonymous biographer. They all failed to see it.

And yet, in the fourteenth or fifteenth century, an equal-armed, cloisonné-celled cross was seen in Durham, and someone thought that the pilgrims and visitors who gazed at it might want to buy a representation of it to show off their travels to the world. So what cross could it have been?

Could the Cuthbert Cross be one of the reliquaries that was once known as the Black Rood, brought to Scotland by Margaret, adopted by Malcolm III, honoured by David I, captured by Edward I, gifted by Edward III, hidden from Edward VI and his father, misattributed by Claxton, found by Gilly and Raine, confirmed by Gary Bankhead?

No record of the Black Rood's destruction exists, its final description is not credible. It exists therefore in limbo, mid-way between the obliterated Croes Gneth and the resurrected Cross of Cong. Perhaps it still exists somewhere, waiting.

David Willem
January 2022

BIBLIOGRAPHY

SCOTLAND AND THE BLACK ROOD

N. B. Aitchison, *Scotland's Stone of Destiny: myth, history and nationhood* (Tempus, 2000).

Joseph Ayloffe, *Calendars of the ancient charters, and of the Welch and Scotish rolls, now remaining in the Tower of London* (Benjamin White, 1774).

Joseph Bain, *Calendar Of Documents Relating to Scotland Preserved In Her Majesty's Public Record Office, London* (General Register Office (Scotland), 1881).

G. W. S. Barrow, *The kingdom of the Scots: government, church and society from the eleventh to the fourteenth century* (Edward Arnold, 1973).

G. W. S. Barrow, *Kingship and Unity: Scotland 1000–1306* (Edward Arnold, 1981).

G. W. S. Barrow, *David I of Scotland (1124–1153): the balance of new and old* (University of Reading, Stenton lecture, 1984).

G. W. S. Barrow, *Robert Bruce & the community of the realm of Scotland* (Edinburgh University Press, 1988).

G. W. S. Barrow, *The charters of King David I: the written acts of David I King of Scots, 1124–53 and of his son Henry Earl of Northumberland, 1139–52* (Boydell Press, 1999).

G. W. S. Barrow, 'Malcolm III', *Oxford Dictionary of National Biography* (OUP, 2004–16).

G. W. S. Barrow, 'Margaret', *Oxford Dictionary of National Biography* (OUP, 2004–16).

David Breeze, Thomas Owen Clancy, Richard Welander, *The Stone of Destiny: artefact and icon* (Society of Antiquaries of Scotland, 2003).

Dauvit Broun, *The Irish identity of the kingdom of the Scots in the twelfth and thirteenth centuries* (Boydell Press, 1999).

Charles Burnett, Christopher Tabraham, *The Honours of Scotland: the story of the Scottish crown jewels* (Historic Scotland, 1993).

R. W. Chambers, Edith C. Batho, H. Winifred Husbands, *The Chronicles of Scotland Compiled by Hector Boece and Translated into Scots by John Bellenden* (Scottish Text Society, Third Series, Vol. 10 & Vol. 15).

Samuel Cowan, *Life of the Princess Margaret, Queen of Scotland, 1070–1093* (Swan & Morgan, 1911).

A. A. M. Duncan, *The Kingship of the Scots, 842–1292: succession and independence* (Edinburgh University Press, 2002).

William Forbes-Leith, *Life of St. Margaret, Queen of Scotland* (William Paterson, 1884).

Jane Patricia Freeland, *Aelred of Rievaulx: the historical works* (Cistercian Publications, 2005).

Richard Gameson, 'The Gospels of Margaret of Scotland and the Literacy of an Eleventh-Century Queen', *Women and the Book* (University of Toronto Press, 1997).

Julianna Grigg, 'The Black Rood of Scotland: a social and political life', *Viator* Vol. 47, Issue 3 (September 2017).

C. Keene, *Saint Margaret, Queen of the Scots: a life in perspective* (Palgrave Macmillan, 2013).

SangDong Lee, *The Development of Dunfermline Abbey as a Royal Cult Centre c.1070–c.1420* (University of Stirling PhD Thesis, 2014).

Neil McGuigan, *Neither Scotland nor England: Middle Britain, c.850–1150* (University of St Andrews PhD Thesis, 2015).

Neil McGuigan, *Mael Coluim III, 'Canmore': an eleventh-century Scottish king* (Birlinn, 2021).

Neil McGuigan, Alex Woolf, *The Battle of Carham: a thousand years on* (John Donald, 2018).

Richard Oram, *David I: the King who made Scotland* (Tempus, 2004).

Michael Penman, 'Christian Days and Knights: the religious devotions and court of David II of Scotland', *Historical Research* Vol. 75, Issue 189 (August, 2002).

Michael Penman, *David II, 1329–71* (John Donald, 2005).

Michael Penman, 'Royal Piety in Thirteenth-Century Scotland: the religion and religiosity of Alexander II (1214–49) and Alexander III (1249–86)', *Thirteen*

Century England XII: proceedings of the Gregynog Conference (Boydell and Brewer, 2009).

Sharla Race, *Aelred of Rievaulx: Cistercian monk and Medieval man: a twelfth century life* (Tigmor Books, 2011).

William Robertson, *Index* (Murray & Cochrane, 1798).

Rebecca Rushforth, *St. Margaret's Gospel Book: the favourite book of an eleventh-century queen* (The Bodleian Library, 2007).

E. L. G. Stones, *Anglo-Scottish relations, 1174–1328: some selected documents* (Clarendon Press, 1970).

E. L. G. Stones, 'Alusion to the Black Rood of Scotland in 1346', *The Scottish Historical Review* Vol. 38, No. 126 (Oct., 1959).

Alice Taylor, 'Historical Writing in Twelfth and Thirteenth Century Scotland, the Dunfermline Compilation', *The Bulletin of the Institute of Historical Research* Vol. 83 (2010).

T. Thomson, C. Innes, *The Acts of the Parliament of Scotland* (British Parliamentary Publications, 1875).

Tom Turpie, 'A Monk from Melrose? St Cuthbert and the Scots in the later middle ages', *The Innes Review* Vol. 62, Issue. 1 (2011).

Ian Walker, *Lords of Alba: the making of Scotland* (Sutton Publishing, 2006).

George Watson, 'The Black Rood of Scotland', *Transactions of the Scottish Ecclesiological Society* Vol. 2 (1906).

MEDIEVAL ENGLAND AND THE BLACK ROOD

Gary Bankhead, *Artefact Report – Pectoral Cross, Pilgrim Souvenir* (Department of Archeology, Durham University, February 2012).

Richard Barber, *The Life and Campaigns of the Black Prince, from contemporary letters, diaries and chronicles, including Chandos Herald's Life of the Black Prince* (Boydell, 1997).

Frank Barlow, 'William II', *Oxford Dictionary of National Biography* (OUP, 2004–16).

Anthony Bash, *Thomas Hatfield: bishop, soldier, and politician* (Institute of Mediaeval and Renaissance Studies, Durham University, 2012).

Nicola Coldstream, Peter Draper, *Medieval Art and Architecture at Durham Cathedral* (British Archaeological Association, 1980).

Joanna Dale, *Inauguration and Liturgical Kingship in the Long Twelfth Century* (York Medieval Press, 2021).

Patricia DeMarco, 'An Arthur for the Ricardian Age: crown, nobility, and the alliterative "Morte Arthure"', *Speculum* Vol. 80, No. 2 (April., 2005).

C. M. Fraser, *A History of Antony Bek, Bishop of Durham, 1283–1311* (Clarendon Press, 1957).

Maxwell Herbert, *The Chronicle of Lanercost, 1272–1346* (J. Maclehose, 1913).

George R. Keiser, 'Edward III and the Aliterative Morte Arthure', *Speculum* Vol. 48, No. 1 (Jan., 1973).

James Ingram, 'The Saxon Chronicle' (Longman, 1823).

Ernest J. B. Kirtlan (trans.), *Sir Gawain and the Green Knight, Rendered Literally into Modern English from the Alliterative Romance-Poem of A.D. 1360, from Cotton MS. Nero A x in British Museum* (Charles H. Kelly, 1912).

Roger Sherman Loomis, 'Edward I, Arthurian enthusiast', *Speculum* Vol. 28, No. 1 (January, 1953).

Julian Munby, Richard Barber, Richard Brown, *Edward III's Round Table at Windsor: the house of the round table and the Windsor festival of 1344* (Boydell, 2007).

W. M. Ormrod, *Symposium on England in the Thirteenth Century* (Paul Watkins Publishing, 1991).

W. M. Ormrod, *Edward III* (Yale University Press, 2011).

Geoffrey Haward Martin, *Knighton's Chronicle 1337–1396* (Clarendon Press, 1995).

Ranald Nicholson, *Edward III and the Scots: the formative years of a military career, 1327–1335* (OUP, 1965).

Michael Prestwich, *Edward I* (Yale University Press, 1997).

Ad Putter, *Sir Gawain and the Green Knight and French Arthurian romance* (Clarendon Press, 1995).

David Rollason and Michael Prestwich (eds.), *The Battle of Neville's Cross* (Shaun Tyas, 1998).

Nigel Saul, Tim Tatton Brown, *St George's Chapel Windsor, History and Heritage* (Dovecote, 2010).

E. L. G. Stones, *Edward I and the Throne of Scotland, 1290–1296: an edition of the record sources for the Great Cause* (Glasgow University Press, 1978).

Philippa Turner, 'The Rood in the Late Medieval English Cathedral', *The Rood in Medieval Britain and Ireland, c. 800–c. 1500* (Boydell Press, 2020).

Juliet Vale, *Edward III and Chivalry: chivalric society and its context, 1270–1350* (Boydell Press, 1982).

Fiona Watson, *Under the Hammer: Edward I and Scotland, 1286–1306* (Tuckwell, 1998).

IRELAND AND THE CROSS OF CONG

Edward Lhuyd, *Archaeologia Britannica* (Oxford, 1707).

John A. Claffey, 'A Very Puzzling Irish Missal', *Journal of the Galway Archaeological and Historical Society*, Vol. 55 (2003).

Richard Ellmann, *Oscar Wilde* (Alfred Knopf, 1988).

Griffin Murray, *The Cross of Cong: a masterpiece of medieval Irish art* (Irish Academic Press, 2014).

Caesar Otway, *A Tour in Connnaught: comprising sketches of Clonmacnoise, Joyce country and Achill* (William Curry and Co., 1839).

Pádraig Ó Riain, Griffin Murray, 'The Cross of Cong: some recent discoveries', *Archaeology Ireland*, Vol. 19, No. 1 (Spring 2005).

George Petrie, 'An account of the Cross of Cong', *Proceedings of the Royal Irish Academy*, Vol. 4 (10 June 1850).

Robert Scott, *Around and About Cong, an introduction to the village of Cong, County Mayo* (Kinlough Press, 2017).

William Stokes, *The Life and Labours in Art and Archaeology of George Petrie* (Longmans, Green and Company, 1868).

Wiliam Wilde, *Lough Corrib, its shores and islands* (McGlashan and Gill, 1867).

WALES AND Y GROES GNETH

R. R. Davies, *Conquest, Coexistence, and Change: Wales, 1063–1415* (Clarendon Press, 1987).

Edward VI, *Chronicle* (ScreamReel Classics Amazon, 2021).

John Edward Morris, *The Welsh Wars of Edward I: a contribution to medieval military history, based on original documents* (Clarendon Press, 1969).

Heather Pagan, 'Word of the Month: the Croes Naid', *Anglo-Norman Dictionary* (accessed September, 2022).

Winifred Coombe Tennant, 'Croes Naid', *National Library of Wales Journal* Vol. 7, No. 2 (Winter, 1951).

MEDIEVAL ENGLAND AND SAINT CUTHBERT

Max Adams, *The King in the North, the life and times of Oswald of Northumbria* (Head of Zeus, 2014).

William M. Aird, *St Cuthbert and the Normans: The Church of Durham, 1071–1153* (Boydell Press, 1998).

William M. Aird, 'St Cuthbert, the Scots and the Normans', *XVI Proceedings of the Battle Conference on Anglo-Norman Studies* (Boydell Press, 1993).

Anon., 'The Wilton Cross: Where was it found?' *St Edmundsbury website* (accessed April, 2007).

Janet Backhouse, Leslie Webster, D. H. Turner, *The Golden Age of Anglo-Saxon Art, 966–1066* (British Museum Publications, 1984).

John Beckwith, *Ivory Carvings in Early Medieval England* (Harvey, Miller and Medcalf, 1972).

Barbara Baert, *A Heritage of Holy Wood: the legend of the True Cross in text and image* (Brill, 2004).

Robert Bartlett, 'Turgot', *Oxford Dictionary of National Biography* (OUP, 2004–16).

C. F. Battiscombe, ed., *The Relics of Saint Cuthbert: Studies by Various Authors* (Oxford University Press, 1956).

Alex Bayliss, Marion Archibald and John Hines, *Anglo-Saxon graves and grave goods of the 6th and 7th centuries AD: a chronological framework* (Society for Medieval Archaeology, 2013).

John Bliese, 'Saint Cuthbert and War', *Journal of Medieval History* Vol, 24, Issue 3 (1998).

Mary-Catherine Bodden, *The Finding of the True Cross* (I.D.S. Brewer, 1987).

Gerald Bonner, David Rollason and Clare Stancliffe (eds.), *St Cuthbert, His Cult and His Community to AD 1200* (Boydell Press, 1989).

Diana Boyson, *The Coffins of Saint Cuthbert* (Durham PhD Thesis, 1974).

David Brown, *Durham Cathedral: history, fabric, and culture* (Yale University Press, 2014).

Peter Brown, *The Cult of the Saints: its rise and function in Latin Christianity* (University of Chicago Press, 1981).

Jo Buckberry, Annia Cherryson, *Burial in later Anglo-Saxon England c. 650–1100 AD* (Oxbow, 2010).

Eric Cambridge, 'Reconsidering Cuthbert's Relics', *The St Cuthbert Gospel: studies on the insular manuscript of the Gospel of John* (British Library, 2015).

Galit Noga-Banai, 'Visual Rhetoric of Early Christian Reliquaries', William R. Caraher, Thomas W. Davis, David K. Pettegrew, *The Oxford Handbook of Early Christian Reliquaries* (OUP, 2019).

Bertram Colgrave, *The Life of Bishop Wilfrid* (Cambridge University Press, 1927).

Bertram Colgrave, *Two Lives of Saint Cuthbert: a life by an anonymous monk of Lindisfarne and Bede's prose life* (Cambridge University Press, 1940).

Robert Colls, *Northumbria: History and Identity 547–2000* (The History Press, 2007).

Margaret Coombe, Anne Mouron, Christiania Whitehead, *Saints of North-East England, 600–1500* (Turnhout, 2017).

J. M. Cronyn and C. V. Horie, *Saint Cuthbert's Coffin* (Durham Cathedral, 1985).

Francesca Dell'Acqua, 'The Carbunculus (Red Garnet) and the Double Nature of Christ in the Early Medieval West', *Journal of Art History* Vol. 86, No. 3 (2017).

Norman Emery, 'The Remains and Relics of Saint Cuthbert', *Durham Cathedral Archaeology Report 23* (2004).

C. Eyre, *The History of Saint Cuthbert* (London, 1887).

Richard Gameson, *The Role of Art in the Late Anglo-Saxon church* (Clarendon Press, 1995).

John Allen Giles, *The Biographical Writing and Letters of Venerable Bede* (Bohn, 1845).

Lionel Green, *Building St Cuthbert's Shrine: Durham Cathedral and the life of Prior Turgot* (Sacristy, 2013).

Cynthia Hahn, 'Collector and Saint: Queen Radegund and the devotion to the relic of the True Cross', *Word & Image* Vol. 22, No. 3 (July–September, 2006).

Catherine Hills, 'Work Boxes or Reliquaries? Small copper-alloy containers in seventh century Anglo-Saxon graves', Stuart Brookes, Sue Harrington, Andrew Reynolds, *Studies in Early Anglo-Saxon Art and Archaeology: papers in honour of Martin G. Welch* (Archaeopress, 2011).

Nicholas Hooper, 'Edgar Aetheling', *Oxford Dictionary of National Biography* (OUP, 2004–16).

John James, 'The Rib Vaults of Durham Cathedral', *Gesta* Vol. 22, No. 2 (1983).

Catherine Karkov, *The Art of Anglo-Saxon England* (Bodyell Press, 2011).

Sarah Larratt Keefer, Karen Louise Jolly, Catherine E. Karkov (eds), *Cross and Cruciform in the Anglo-Saxon World* (West Virginia University Press, 2010).

T. D. Kendrick, 'St Cuthbert's Pectoral Cross, and the Wilton and Ixworth Crosses', *The Antiquaries Journal* Vol. 17, Issue 3 (July, 1937).

Sam Lucy, 'The Trumpington Cross in Context', *Anglo-Saxon England* Vol. 45 (December, 2016).

Arthur MacGregor, 'A Seventh-Century Pectroral Cross from Holdeness, East Yorkshire', *Medieval Archeology* Vol. 44 (2000).

Arthur MacGregor, 'The Holderness Anglo-Saxon Cross', *Minerva 3* Vol. 2. No, 2 (March/April, 2000).

Annemarie Mahler, 'Lignum Domini and the Opening Vision of the Dream of the Rood: a viable hypothesis?' *Speculum* Vol. 53, No. 3 (July 1978).

Dominic Marner, *St. Cuthbert: His Life and Cult in Medieval Durham* (British Library, 2000).

John Munns, *Cross and Culture in Anglo-Norman England: theology, imagery, devotion* (Boydell Press, 2016).

C. Peers and C.A. Ralegh Radford, 'The Saxon Monastery at Whitby', *Archaeologia 89* (1943).

Barbara Catherine Raw, *Anglo-Saxon Crucifixion Iconography and the Art of the Monastic Revival* (Cambridge University Press, 1990).

Barbara Catherine Raw, 'The Dream of the Rood and its connections with early Christian Art', *Medium Aevum* Vol. 39, No. 3 (1970).

David Rollason, ed., *Cuthbert: Saint and Patron* (Dean and Chapter of Durham, 1987).

David Rollason, Margaret Harvey and Michael Prestwich (eds.), *Anglo-Norman Durham 1093–1193* (Boydell Press, 1994).

David Rollason, *Simeon of Durham: historian of Durham and the north* (Tyas Studies in North-Eastern history, 1998).

David Rollason (ed.), *Symeon of Durham: Libellus de Exordio atque Procursu istius, hoc est Dunhelmensis, Ecclesie* (Clarendon Press, 2000).

Ilse A Schweitzer, 'The Crux Gemmata and Shifting Significances of the Cross in Insular Art', *Marginalia: The Journal of the Medieval Reading Group at the University of Cambridge* (2006).

Richard Sharpe, 'Banners of the Northern Saints', *Proceedings of the Saints of the North of England 600–1500 Conference* (2015)

E. A. Slater, 'White Inlays in Anglo-Saxon Jewelry', *Science and Archeology Glasgow 1987: conference on the application of scientific techniques to archeology* (1987).

Ted Johnson South, *Historia De Sancto Cuthberti: a history of Saint Cuthbert and a record of his patrimony* (D.S. Brewer, 2001).

Michael Swanton, *The Dream of the Rood* (Manchester University Press, 1970).

Michael Swanton, *The Anglo-Saxon Chronicle* (Phoenix, 2000).

Nicholas Vincent, *The Holy Blood: King Henry III and the Westminster blood relic* (Cambridge University Press, 2001).

J. Warren, 'Saxon remains found near Ixworth', *Collectanae Antiqua* Vol. 4, p. 162.

J. F. Webb, *The Age of Bede* (Penguin, 1988).

J. Werner, 'Frankish Royal Tombs in the Cathedrals of Cologne and Saint Denis', *Antiquity* Vol. 38 (1964).

Post-medieval Durham

Richard Bailey, Eric Cambridge, 'St Cuthbert's Posthumous Biography: a revised edition', *Peritia* Vol, 26 (2015).

William Brown, 'Saint Cuthbert's Grave and Coffin', *The Ushaw Magazine 9* (1899).

William Brown, 'Saint Cuthbert's Remains', *The Ushaw Magazine 19* (1909).

William Claxton, *The Rites of Durham* (the Surtees Society and the Catholic Record Society, Boydell Press, 2020).

J. T. Fowler, 'On an Examination of the Grave of Saint Cuthbert', *Archaeologia 57* (1900).

George William Kitchin, 'The Contents of Saint Cuthbert's Shrine', *The Victoria History of the Counties of England: Durham* (Archibald Constable & Co., 1905).

John Lingard, *Remarks on the 'Saint Cuthbert' of the Rev. James Raine, M.A.* (Newcastle, 1828).

Christian Liddy, *The Bishopric of Durham in the Late Middle Ages: lordship, community and the cult of St Cuthbert* (Boydell Press, 2008).

Phillip Lindley, *Tomb Destruction and Scholarship: medieval monuments in early modern England* (Shaun Tyas, 2007).

Robert McCombe, 'Two Exhumations and an Attempted Theft: the posthumous biography of St Cuthbert in the Nineteenth Century and its historicist narratives', *Archeological Journal* Vol. 171, Issue 1 (2014).

Geoffrey Moorhouse, *The Last Office: 1539 and the dissolution of a monastery* (Phoenix, 2009).

Hugh Norwood, Nicholas Groves, *William Stephen Gilly: an exceptionally busy life* (Lasse Press, 2014).

Connor O'Brien, 'Attitudes to St Cuthbert's Body during the Nineteenth Century', *Northern History* Vol. 53, Issue 2 (2016).

James Raine, *Saint Cuthbert: with an account of the state in which his remains were found upon the opening of his tomb in Durham Cathedral, in the year MDCCCXXVII* (Geoffrey Andrews, 1828).

NOTES: REFERENCES AND DESCRIPTIONS RELATING TO THE BLACK ROOD OF SCOTLAND

1   **Vita (Life of St Magaret) c. 1100.** This is the earliest reference to the Black Rood. The *Vita* is generally considered to have been written by Turgot, and three manuscript versions have survived: *Cotton Tiberius Diii* (British Library, last quarter of twelfth century); an abbreviated *Cotton Tiberius Ei* (British Library, fourteenth century); and the *Dunfermline Vita* (Madrid, from early in the reign of Alexander III 1249–86). There is also a copy in *Acta Sanctorum*, which is an edition of the lost Vaucelles manuscript, but this version is identical to *Cotton Tiberius Diii*. The *Vita* contains a description of the Black Rood, however see note *ii* below.

     The translations of Margaret's words on her death bed are from William Forbes-Leith, *Life of St. Margaret, Queen of Scotland* (William Paterson, 1884).

2   **Aelred, *Genealogia regum Anglorum* (Genealogy of the Kings of the English) 1153–54.** The first description of the Black Rood is from Aelred's contemporaneous 'Lament for David, King of Scots' which went on to become the opening chapter of his *Genealogia*, of which there are 22 surviving manuscripts, most of which include the Lament. It is the only eleventh- or twelfth-century description one of the Black Rood, and, as identical wording appears in both Turgot's *Vita* and Aelred's *Genealogia*, the description could have originated in either one or the other, with the consensus being that it was composed by Aelred and then inserted into the *Vita*.

     'The cross, the length of the palm of the hand, was made with surpassing skill out of pure gold; it opens and closes like a box. In it can be seen a portion of the Lord's cross, as had been often proved by the evidence of many miracles. It bears the image of our Saviour carved from the most beautiful ivory and is marvellously adored with golden ornaments. The devout Queen Margaret, the king's mother, who sprang from the royal seed of the English and Hungarians, passed on to her sons as a hereditary gift this cross she brought to Scotland'.

     The translation is from Jane Patricia Freeland, *Aelred of Rievaulx: the historical works* (Cistercian Publications, 2005). (© 2008 by Order of Saint Benedict, Collegeville, Minnesota. Used with permission.)

3   Writing in the 1170s the Durham historian Reginald states that Margaret 'transmitted [willed] to Saint Cuthbert the cross, sparkling in a most wonderful manner with pearls and jewels, which even when dying she held in her hand'. This quotation appears in Reginald's 'Little book' of Cuthbert miracles, the *Libellus de admirandis beati Cuthberti virtutibbus,* although he does not specify that this cross was known as the Black Rood. The translation is from George Watson, 'The Black Rood of Scotland', *Transactions of the Scottish Ecclesiological Society* Vol. 2 (1906) p. 32.

4   *An indenture of the muniments taken possession of in the Treasury of Edinburgh and deposited at Berwick, in the year 1291, by the command of the English King* **August, 1291.** This inventory of Scotland's charters and treasures was composed when they were transferred into the custody of Edward I while he adjudicated on the Great Cause. It includes the following section heading and item description.

'All those were found in a certain chest in the dormitory of Holyrood and were again put in the same place by the said abbots and others, under their seals… A silver case covered with gold in which rests the cross which is called the Black Rood'.

The translation is from George Watson, 'The Black Rood of Scotland', *Transactions of the Scottish Ecclesiological Society* Vol. 2 (1906) p. 38. The original Latin can be seen in Robertson's *An index, drawn up about the year 1629, of many records of charters, granted by the different sovereigns of Scotland between the years 1309 and 1413, most of which records have been long missing…* (Murray & Cochrane, 1798) p. xiii. The same entry can also be seen in two other reference works: T. Thomson, C. Innes, *The Acts of the Parliament of Scotland* (British Parliamentary Publications, 1875) Vol.1. Part 1, p. 112; and Joseph Ayloffe, *Calendars of the ancient charters, and of the Welch and Scotish rolls, now remaining in the Tower of London* (Benjamin White, 1774) p. 330.

5 **Letter from Robert Wishart, Bishop of Glasgow, 7 October 1300.** The letter declares that Wishart has renewed his oath of fealty to Edward 'upon the consecrated host, the Holy Evangels, the Cross Neyth and the Black Rood of Scotland'.

Quoted in George Watson, 'The Black Rood of Scotland', *Transactions of the Scottish Ecclesiological Society* Vol. 2 (1906) p. 39. According to Watson, Bishop Wishart swore similar oaths a total of five times. The letter is referenced in Joseph Bain, *Calendar Of Documents Relating to Scotland Preserved In Her Majesty's Public Record Office, London* (General Register Office (Scotland), 1881) Vol. 5, No. 535. This entry includes other references to the swearing of loyalty by Wishart and other Scottish magnates but does not mention the presence of the Black Rood or Y Groes Gneth.

6 **Wardrobe Accounts 1301–4** These records of personal offerings by Edward I demonstrate the significance of the Black Rood and Y Groes Gneth to him.

'On 22nd July 1301, King Edward I made an oblation of seven shillings in the chapel at Kelso, while to the Cross Neyth, the Thorn or Spine, and the Black Rood were offered five shillings, three shillings and three shillings respectively. On 14th September following he offered to the Cross Neyth, in honour of the holy Cross, the sum of five shillings, while to the Thorn he made an offering of three shillings. On 1st November 1304, Edward made an oblation of the sum of seven shillings at the altar in his own chapel in the manor of Brurstwick; to the Cross Neyth he offered seven shillings, to the Spine of the Crown of Christ three shillings, and to the Black Rood of Scotland two shillings'.

Quoted in George Watson, 'The Black Rood of Scotland', *Transactions of the Scottish Ecclesiological Society* Vol. 2 (1906) p. 40.

7 **The Inventory of Relics made at Burgh on Sands, 17 July 1307.** This was drawn up ten days after Edward I died at Burgh on Sands while on his way to re-attempt the subjugation of Scotland, thus showing that, like David I, he kept the Black Rood near him.

'In a casket marked with the sign of the cross… la Blakrode of Scotland, of gold-work with a gold chain, in a wooden case with silver-gilt exterior. Item crux Sancte Elene de Scot of gold-work and gems, in a case of wood and leather… A box (*teca*) of silver gilt and gems containing part of the Holy Cross and many small relics of the confessor St Edmund, in a burse bearing the arms of the king of France, with other relics which that king sent to Alexander, king of Scotland, that were found in Edinburgh castle, all in a leather case'.

The source is Joseph Bain, *Calendar Of Documents Relating to Scotland Preserved In Her Majesty's Public Record Office, London* (General Register Office (Scotland), 1881) Vol. 5, No. 494.

8 **Chronicle of Lanercost, mid-Fourteenth Century.** The contemporaneous source for the claim that the Black Rood was returned to Scotland by the young Edward III following the disastrous Battle of Stanhope and the 1328 Treaty of Edinburgh (Northampton).

'…acting on the pestilent advice of his mother and Sir Roger de Mortimer (they being the chief controllers of the king, who was barely fifteen years of age) he was forced to release the Scots by his public deed from all exaction, right, claim or demand of the overlordship of the kingdom of Scotland on his part, and that of his heirs and successors in perpetuity, and from any homage to be done to the Kings of England. He restored to them also that piece of the Cross of Christ which the Scots call the Black Rood…'

Translation from Maxwell Herbert, *The Chronicle of Lanercost, 1272–1346* (J. Maclehose, 1913) pp. 259–60. Sixteenth-century chroniclers such as Fabyan and Holinshed were to repeat the claim that the Black Rood was returned to Scotland. However, although the Lanercost chronicler was writing just after the Battle of Neville's Cross in 1346, he does not mention the re-capture of the Black Rood at the battle. Nor does any other contemporaneous source.

9   **English Treasury Memorandum, 7 January 1346.** This record is unreconcilable with the return of the Black Rood claimed in the Lanercost Chronicle (see note viii).

'...on this date the Blackrood of Scotland was taken from the Tower of London and delivered to Walter de Wetewang, keeper of the wardrobe, to be kept by the king's side.'

This memorandum can no longer be found but is noted in Palgrave's *Kalendars* I. 160 as per Joseph Bain, *Calendar Of Documents Relating to Scotland Preserved In Her Majesty's Public Record Office, London* (General Register Office (Scotland), 1881) Vol. 5, No. 800.

There is also a document dated 12 April 1344 which may be relevant: 'Two indentures listing the relics, [etc.]. delivered to William de Edyngdon, treasurer, by his predecessor, William de Cusaunce... among them bones of St Magaret, Queen of Scotland. Also listed in 'a sliver-gilt cross, with a part in the middle of black wood'.

The source is Joseph Bain, *Calendar Of Documents Relating to Scotland Preserved In Her Majesty's Public Record Office, London* (General Register Office (Scotland), 1881) Vol. 5, No. 799.

10 **The Durham Shrine Keeper's List, 1383.** The earliest reference to the Black Rood in Durham, the inventory was drawn up following the installation of the Neville Screen or reredos (altar screen) which commemorated the death of one of the English commanders at the Battle of Neville's Cross. It is conceivable that the 'steps' referred to in the list are actually the display plinths on the rear of the reredos, although it is generally accepted that they refer to shelves in the display cases around the shrine.

'In the year of our Lord 1383... this book was composed of the relics in the shrine of the saint.... by Sir Thomas Segbruk, then keeper of the shrine, in order to declare what and of what nature the relics... in what place, or upon what step. In primis: in the first or highest step to the south, an image of the blessed virgin Mary, of silver gilt. Item, and image of... of silver gilt, with a rib of the same, enclosed in the breast of the image. Item: a black cross called the Black Rode of Scotland.'

Translation in James Raine, *Saint Cuthbert: with an account of the state in which his remains were found upon the opening of his tomb in Durham Cathedral, in the year MDCCCXXVII* (Geoffrey Andrews, 1828) p. 121.

11 **The Rites of Durham, 1597** The final document concerning the Black Rood is an unfinished description of the pre-Reformation cathedral at Durham. *Rites* describes the architecture, fixtures, fittings and ornamentation in and around the cathedral, detailing some of the building's ancient and recent history. It was originally thought to have been written by a former monk, George Bates, but contemporary research has confirmed the author as William Claxton. A number of manuscipt and published versions exist based on various manuscripts by Claxton only one of which survives. For a full discussion, see Margaret Harvey and Lynda Rollason's new edition: William Claxton, *The Rites of Durham* (the Surtees Society and the Catholic Record Society, Boydell Press, 2020). For simplicity, the page references below relate to this edition, while the transcriptions themselves originate from an earlier edition having also been adusted to correspond with modern orthography.

Rites has three elements that deal with the Black Rood.

1. **A description of the Battle of Neville's Cross, which had happened over 200 years before, including a version of the legend of the origin of the Black Rood in which David II is mistaken for David I.**

'In which said battle, a holy cross which was taken out of the Holy Roodhouse in Edinburgh in Scotland by King David Bruce was won and taken upon the said King of Scotland at the said battle, which cross by most ancient and credible writers is recorded to have come to the King most miraculously, and to have happened and chanced into his hand being a hunting at the wild hart in the forest near Edinburgh upon Holy Rood day, commonly called the exaltation of the cross, the said King separated and parted from his nobles and company, suddenly there appeared unto him as it seemed a most fair hart running towards him in a full and speedy course, which so afraid the king's horse, that he violently coursed away, whom the hart so fiercely and swiftly followed, that he bore forcibly both the King and his horse to ground who so being dismayed did cast back his hand betwixt the tynds of the said hart to stay himself and then and there more strangely slipped into the King's hands the said cross most wondrously, at the view whereof immediately the hart vanished away, and never after was seen. No man knowing certainly what metal or wood the said cross was made of. In the place where the miracle was so wrought doth now spring a fountain called the Rood Well. And the next night after the said cross so bechanced unto him, the said King was charged and warned in his sleep by a vision to build an abbey in the same place which he most diligently observing as a true message from God almighty did send for workmen into France and Flanders who at their coming were retained and did build and erect the said abbey accordingly which the King caused to be furnished with canons regular and dedicated the same in the honour of the Cross and placed the said Cross most sumptuously and richly in the said abbey there to remain as a most renowned monument. And so there remained till the said King coming towards the said battle did bring it upon him as a most miraculous and fortunate relic'. pp. 151-2.

2. **The institutional memory of the ceremony in which the Black Rood was gifted to the cathedral following the Battle of Neville's Cross.**

'And after many conflict and warlike exploits there had been done between the English and the King of Scots and his company, the said battle ended and the victory was obtained...' p. 149.

'In which battle were slain seven earls of Scotland, besides many earls and Scottish men, to the number of one and fifteen thousand, but also lost the said cross. Which was taken upon him, and many together most worthy and excellent jewels and monuments which were brought from Scotland, as his own banner and other noblemen's ancients [banners]. Which all were offered up at the shrine of St Cuthbert for the beautifying and adoring thereof, together with the Black Rood of Scotland (so termed)...' pp. 153-4.

'The King of Scots Ancient and his banner with the Lord Neville's banner, and diverse other noblemen's ancients were all brought to St Cuthbert's feretory (shrine), and there the said Lord Neville after the battle done in most solemn and humble manner did make his petition to God and that holy man St Cuthbert within the feretory to accept his offerings and did offer the aforesaid jewels and banners and the holy rood cross which was taken on the King of Scots to the shrine of that holy and blessed man St Cuthbert within the Feretory; and so after his orisons performed to God and St Cuthbert he departed and there the said banners and ancients did stand, and hung until the suppression of the house...' p. 106.

3. **A description of the Black Rood before it disappeared in the Reformation**

'At the east end of the south alley, adjoining to the pillar next St Cuthbert's feretory, next to the choir door on the south side, there was a most fair rood or picture of our Saviour, called the Black Rood of Scotland with the picture of Mary and John being brought out of Holyrood house in Scotland by King David Bruce, and was won at the battle of Durham with the picture of our lady on one side of our Saviour and the picture of St John on the other side, the which Rood and pictures were all three very richly wrought in silver, the which were all smoked black over, being large pictures of a yard and five quarters long, and on every one of their heads, a crown of pure beaten gold of goldsmith's work with a device or rest to take them off or on. And on the backside of the said rood and pictures, there was a piece of work that they were fastened unto being all adorned with fine wainscot work and curious paintings well befitting such costly pictures from the middle pillar up to the height of the vault, the which wainscot was all red varnished over very finely, and all set full of stars of lead, every star finely gilded over with gold, and also the said rood and pictures had every of them an iron stuck fast in the back part of the said images that had a hole in the said irons, that went through the wainscot to put in a pin of iron to make them fast to the wainscot.' pp. 139-40.